on track ...
Level 42

every album, every song

Matt Phillips

sonicbondpublishing.com

Sonicbond Publishing Limited
www.sonicbondpublishing.co.uk
Email: info@sonicbondpublishing.co.uk

First Published in the United Kingdom 2021
First Published in the United States 2021

British Library Cataloguing in Publication Data:
A Catalogue record for this book is available from the British Library

Copyright Matt Phillips 2021

ISBN 978-1-78952-102-3

Typeset in ITC Garamond & ITC Avant Garde
Printed and bound in England

Graphic design and typesetting: Full Moon Media

on track ...

Level 42

every album, every song

Matt Phillips

sonicbondpublishing.com

Acknowledgements

Special thanks to Mark King, who kindly answered my questions about his first solo album *Influences*; Gary Husband, Phil Gould and Paul Waller for their valued contributions; Nathan King; Simon Gurney; Stephen Lambe; William Ellis; Jez Crowther; James Hayes; Johnny Chandler; Alex Myers; Steve Khan; Phill Brown; Chris Dancy; Steve Hammonds; David Webb; Julian Hall; George Cole; James McGowan; Bill Milkowski; Jem Godfrey, Duncan Dodds and Alex Evans for fun times playing air bass to 'Sandstorm'; my brother Jon for the jam sessions; my parents Viviane and Michael for their love and support; and of course Mark, Mike, Boon, Phil, Wally, Gary and Allan H for the great music and memories.

This book is dedicated to James Broad.

on track ...

Level 42

Contents

Foreword 9
The Early Days: 1955-1979 13
1980: The Birth Of The Band 19
The Early Tapes (1980) 20
Level 42 (1981) 27
The Pursuit Of Accidents (1982) 35
Standing In The Light (1983) 42
Influences (Mark King solo) (1984) 51
True Colours (1984) 56
A Physical Presence (1985) 65
World Machine (1985) 72
Running In The Family (1987) 80
Interlude: 1989 97
Changes (Mike Lindup solo) (1990) 98
Guaranteed (1991) 102
Interlude: 1992-1994 111
Forever Now (1994) 112
Interlude 1994-2006 119
Retroglide (2006) 121
Interlude (2007-2012) 125
Sirens EP (2013) 128
Postscript 131
Selected Official Compilations/Box Sets 133
Selected Official DVDs/Videos 134
Selected Online/TV/Radio References: 136
Bibliography 141

Foreword

29 April 2019: social media is ablaze with the news that Boon Gould – co-founder, guitarist and lyricist for Level 42 – has died. It's a sad farewell to the original line-up of one of the most successful and iconic British bands of the 1980s. Their prestigious catalogue spans a seldom-documented, golden period for pop, and it may not even be so outlandish to suggest they defined that musical decade in the same way as Steely Dan did the 1970s and The Beatles the 1960s.

The band's effervescent hits 'Something About You' and 'Lessons In Love' were two of the most ubiquitous tunes of the era. Consequently they somehow became synonymous with Thatcher's decade, supposedly the favourite of yuppies and young 'Loadsamoneys'-about-town. Far from reflecting any political leanings, this was down to the effortless brilliance of their music and also their relative 'facelessness' as a brand; Level 42 never graced the covers of *The Face, BLITZ* or *i-D*. But their pop period also tended to obscure the band's roots as a first-rate jazz/rock/funk unit; even at their commercial peak, they were smuggling Stanley Clarke and Mahavishnu Orchestra licks into the charts, and chief lyricist/drummer Phil Gould was referencing highbrow works by Arthur Koestler, Hermann Hesse and E.M. Forster. In the memorable words of *Q Magazine*'s Phil Sutcliffe, Level 42 were the 'musical equivalent of fusing *The Sun* and *The Guardian*', the ultimate 'fusion' band, streamlining high-octane jazz/rock into slick, soulful pop.

Bassist/lead vocalist Mark King was one of the most visible homegrown pop stars of the mid-to-late-1980s, world-famous for the furious slapping of his Jaydee Supernatural bass and press reports of Polydor Records insuring his right thumb to the tune of three million pounds. But he was also a world-class drummer, excellent songwriter and singer. In terms of pure talent, you could make a case that in the field of British 'pop' artists, his musicianship is second to none. And although Mark's 'thunderthumb' was apparently the band's USP, any fan will tell you that it was only a small part of Level 42's DNA. Also very much in the mix were the effervescent pop melodies of Todd Rundgren, Paul McCartney and James Taylor, hard funk grooves of James Brown and Sly & The Family Stone, progressive sounds of King Crimson, Yes and Genesis, mellow vibes of The Band, Lindisfarne and Fairport Convention, and classic fusion of *Bitches Brew*-era Miles Davis, Weather Report and Return To Forever.

I won't forget the first time Level 42 appeared on my radar. It was 27 January 1983 and, like millions of other young people across the UK, I was watching the BBC's flagship pop show *Top Of The Pops*. The band were miming their latest hit 'The Chinese Way' but didn't look or sound like anything else from the era. They had a punky energy and some otherworldly synth sounds courtesy of Mike Lindup and Wally Badarou, all undercut by the phenomenal rhythm section of Mark, guitarist Boon Gould and his brother Phil on drums.

Cut to 13 July 1985, the day of *Live Aid*. I was now a burgeoning musician and nascent album buyer, and, during a trip to the Virgin Megastore on Oxford

Street, bought the band's live double record *A Physical Presence*. It was my proper introduction to Level's music and I was blown away. I excitedly bought all of their earlier albums (and was perfectly primed to witness their pop breakthrough in the autumn of 1985), an absolute treat back in the days when whole swathes of an artist's catalogue could remain a mystery. It was the start of a musical love affair which has lasted over 35 years.

In their original iteration, Level 42 excelled at supplying two musical elements not exactly native to British shores: groove and virtuosity. They had something in common with other funky, homegrown units of the 1970s such as Kokomo, The Blockheads, Average White Band, and later, Shakatak, Morrissey-Mullen, Light Of The World, Incognito and Freeez, but were on a different planet in terms of raw musicianship, melodic sense and rhythmic propulsion. The band were initially nurtured by a readymade 'Britfunk' scene, but it was a scene they had outgrown, even by the time of their first top 40 single 'Love Games'. Though they shared some influences (Herbie Hancock, Lonnie Liston Smith, The Crusaders, P-Funk, Stevie Wonder), they were a far tighter proposition than the other Britfunk bands, with a raw energy and two world-class, jack-in-the-box talents in Mark and Phil. Theirs was a decidedly sparkier, more diverse – though always melodic – version of funk.

But how did they create such an original sound? Three of the band (Mark, Boon and Phil) originated from the Isle Of Wight, an island off the south coast of England, not exactly a funk mecca in the 1960s and 1970s but somewhat of a bohemian outpost. The famous Isle Of Wight Festival of 1970 had certainly put the island on the map (Mark told BBC Radio 1's Andy Peebles in 1984 that he remembers perching himself on a hill near the site and hearing – if not seeing – Jimi Hendrix and Miles Davis' famous sets). Records were not easy to get hold of; you had to order them at one of the few decent shops and hope the right album arrived in the post a few weeks later. In the mid-1970s, a few visual artists were making a good living on the island but not many musicians, though it was a vibrant, popular holiday destination during the summer months, with 'Hoo-ray Henrys' from London or Portsmouth filling the nightclubs, hotels and restaurants, giving seasonal employment to Mark, Phil and Boon.

Then there was the band's musical and cultural good fortune: luckily for Mark, the bass guitar was arguably *the* musical currency of the late-70s/early-80s, with players such as Sting, Louis Johnson, Nick Beggs, Mick Karn, Verdine White, Jah Wobble, Tina Weymouth, Marcus Miller, Jean-Jacques Burnel and Peter Hook giving the instrument huge credibility. Every Britfunk and post-punk band had a notable bass-spanker, and Mark was perfectly placed to tap into the zeitgeist, though he used lighter strings than the aforementioned players and also had far more of a 'drumming' sensibility.

When Level 42 started, punk was still an influence on the UK music scene. As Mark mentioned to *Q Magazine* in 1994, 'If we'd been young guys ten years earlier, we'd have been punks'. (Interestingly, he included songs by The Stranglers and Siouxsie & The Banshees when choosing his top ten for BBC

Radio 1 in 1984). But they were always far more musically proficient and jazz-influenced than 'bona fide' post-punkers such as A Certain Ratio and This Heat. Mark was also inspired by a conversation he had read between Return To Forever's Lenny White and Chick Corea about how there was no 'positivity' in punk, just a lot of complaining. Mark looked around at the picturesque surroundings of the Isle Of Wight and wisely decided against complaining, focusing rather on doing his 10,000 hours and mastering the technicalities of his instrument(s). As author Simon Reynolds points out in his book *Totally Wired,* 'If punk was a destructive response to boredom, you could say that post-punk was a constructive response'.

A lot of Level 42's success was also down to their Janus-like outlook – though often seen as pioneers of recording technology, they were keen to work with experienced producer/engineers such as Mike Vernon, Ken Scott and Jerry Boys, who learnt their trade during the 1960s pop boom. In the 1980s, a lot of store was placed in sonic clarity, but songwriting and arrangements were just as important to Level, as well as personal likeability. As Human League/Buzzcocks/Altered Images producer Martin Rushent says in *Totally Wired,* 'To be a producer in the eighties required a mixture of being an electronics engineer, a computer whiz, a synthesist, a musician, a sound engineer, a diplomat, a psychologist...'.

Their natural musical diversity and inbuilt musicianship also helped. They were essentially a band of four multi-instrumentalists: Phil was proficient on drums, percussion and keyboards, Mike was a fine pianist and percussionist, Mark was a bass/drums/guitar triple-threat, and Boon was at home on guitar, bass or saxophone, and occasionally played keyboards in concert. They also became a true 'songwriters collective', though, arguably, lyricists Phil and Boon were the conscience of the band during their commercial peak; the former brought an interest in esoterica, psychoanalysis and science fiction, the latter always an original take on the love song.

It's also worth remembering that Level 42 were, are, and always have been, primarily a live band, best known for their dynamic concerts. But, as we'll see, their relentless touring commitments also had a positive influence on their recording and songwriting smarts.

Music fans – especially those into progressive rock or jazz/fusion – are usually mindful of their heroes 'selling out'. But if you're going to do it, DO it, and Level did it fantastically. After all, they were not exactly dealing in Mongolian throat-singing before 1985. They always had the building blocks: good melodies, good grooves, strong vocals. It was just a question of arrangement, plus Mark's increasing confidence as a frontman and top-line melody writer. 'Jazz purists accuse us of selling out, but I like the fact that we can do that. Miles Davis was at the cutting edge of music for three decades but I know that he would have given his right arm to have had hit singles', as he told *Q Magazine* in 1994.

At the time of writing, the band is about to embark on its 40th-anniversary tour, and it's also the 40th anniversary of their self-titled debut album. It seems a great time to focus on their illustrious catalogue. So sling on your Jaydee Supernatural and get ready for a deep dive into the work of one of the greatest bands of the 1980s and beyond.

All quotes and recording information have been gleaned from liner notes, personal/print/online interviews and YouTube clips. Readers are heartily encouraged to explore the sources for themselves. And a spoiler alert: there'll be a little musical analysis and basic terminology throughout the text. After all, this band has some serious chops.

The Early Days: 1955-1979

Mark King

Mark King was born on 20 October 1958 in Northwood on the Isle Of Wight. His parents Ray and Bridget were both music fans, his father Ray an occasional drummer. Ray became a prison officer when Mark was two, and the family – including Mark's two elder sisters, Belinda and Rachel – moved into prison lodgings in Camp Hill. Mark doesn't have many memories of these early years apart from getting his 'number one' haircut once a month and starting at Parkhurst Primary School at the age of five. But he didn't enjoy school, and was often sick with nerves, once saying, 'If you ask too many questions, you're not thought of as being bright'. By most accounts he was a decent boxer though – he attended Newport Boxing Club and had won three trophies by the age of ten.

He was a fan of The Rolling Stones and The Beatles and started gravitating towards drumming at around nine, bashing the kitchen saucepans, tin lids and pickle jars. He saw Cream miming 'I Feel Free' on *Top Of The Pops* and remembers bassist/vocalist Jack Bruce making a huge impression on him. He was interested in playing the cello, but was put off by his school: 'They had four cellos which were allotted to brainy kids! I was far too thick for that, good for cannon fodder', he told *Guitarist* magazine in 1991. In 1968, his father spent £10 on Mark's first drum kit; a makeshift affair bought from Graham Eldridge in Newport. Mark started making a notebook of all his instruments, which he continues to do to this day. In 1969, he started guitar lessons with a local chap named Tom Taylor, but the drums were becoming an all-encompassing passion.

A prison Alsatian dog named Dax attacked Mark in October 1969, leaving him with his famously scarred cheek. He started playing in a duet with a guitarist named Colin Gibson in 1970, and they auditioned (unsuccessfully) with Beatles songs for a TV talent show called *Anything You Can Do*. Mark also got his first proper drum kit; a red Pearl set from Teague's in Newport which cost £109. His younger brother and future Level 42 guitarist Nathan was born on 29 August 1970, around the time that Mark got his first electric guitar, a Fender Stratocaster. In 1971, Mark started at Cowes High School and joined the Army Cadet Air Force big band, but frequently ran into trouble when they played 'traditional' jazz compositions of the Ted Heath/Joe Loss variety; his playing was very loud, busy and chaotic, not always geared towards straight-ahead jazz, but he was an absolute whirlwind, an incredible talent who turned heads wherever he played.

In 1971, he joined his first covers band – Pseudo Foot – featuring bassist and early mentor Phil Whittington. They started playing the pub circuit and Mark found himself singing Osmonds songs and even performing for his teachers at The Gurnard Hotel. Pseudo Foot got a review in *The Islander* newspaper, the first time Mark had been named in print.

Then there was another life-changing TV moment in his musical rite of passage: he caught the BBC's *In Concert* programme on 9 September 1972, featuring John McLaughlin and The Mahavishnu Orchestra, completely by chance when pressing the wrong button on his parents' new TV. 'Suddenly there was this guy on a double-necked guitar, another guy with a perspex drum kit and two bass drums, and this psychopathic looking guy on a Fender Rhodes with the top torn off, and this freaky violinist as well. It was fantastic! I just sat there gobsmacked!', Mark told *Guitarist* magazine. It was the start of a love affair with McLaughlin's music:

Such a hero of mine! I loved it when people like (jazz/rock guitar pioneer) Larry Coryell said that being in the same room as him was like being in the same room as Jesus Christ. It absolutely fitted my idea of this guy who was larger than life and did impossible things. I even took an album of his into the hairdressers and said that I wanted my hair cut just like that. Unfortunately, there was also a picture of (Indian spiritual guru) Sri Chimnoy on it as well, with his shaven head. So I ended up looking like one of the cast of (Alan Clarke's 1977 BBC borstal drama) *Scum*!

He excitedly ordered Mahavishnu's *The Inner Mounting Flame* from his nearest record shop in Newport – which then took ten days to arrive. But this revelation led to a newfound obsession with jazz/rock, particularly the drumming of Billy Cobham and bass playing of Stanley Clarke.

In 1973, when Mark was fifteen, he played the lead in the stage version of wartime drama, *The Best Years Of Our Lives,* and appeared in a production of *Camelot* on Sandown Pier. He completed his CSEs and started playing on the island's summer gig circuit, also occasionally giving drum lessons to the children of prison officers. The kit was now an all-consuming passion, and he had the ambition to match. 'When I was sixteen, people would ask, "What do you want to do?". I'd say, I want to be the best drummer in the world', Mark told the *Rapido* TV programme in 1992.

In 1976, he passed his driving test, left school and started working on a farm and in a cigarette lighter factory. He wrote to one of his heroes, drummer Lenny White, asking for career advice, and was delighted to receive a reply with words of encouragement and a home address. It was a red rag to a bull for Mark – he headed for Queens, New York in September 1977 and spent two weeks checking out the music scene and plucking up the courage to knock on Lenny's door. Lenny let him in, gave him a sneak preview of his album *The Adventures Of Astral Pirates* and showed him his two drum kits. It was a thrilling afternoon. Mark was on cloud nine, taking it as a sign that he was moving in the right direction.

In March 1978, he threw the drum kit into the back of his van and set off for London, crashing on his sister Belinda's floor. He got a job at the famous Macari's music shop on the Charing Cross Road, sweeping the floor, doing some DIY, demonstrating basses (they didn't sell drums) and Coloursound effects pedals. Though he was an inexperienced bass player, unsurprisingly he took to the instrument amazingly quickly, tapping into his natural love for Stanley Clarke, Jack Bruce, Jaco Pastorius and Larry Graham, utilising his drumming prowess and also picking up tips from the West End showband players who would come in to try out new instruments.

Mark eventually moved out of his sister's place and into a flatshare in Hammersmith, West London. In the summer of 1979, fate would bring Mark, Mike, Boon and Phil together, and London was the focal point.

Mike Lindup

Michael Lindup was born on 17 March 1959 at Guy's Hospital, Southwark, south-east London (which makes him almost a proper Cockney). His mother, Nadia Cattouse, was born in Belize. She was an actress and pianist who loved soca music, Duke Ellington and Lena Horne. She moved to London to work for the immigration service where she met David Lindup, a successful composer/arranger with a very varied career, including creating a lot of library music (some of which can be heard on the soundtrack of John Carpenter's 1980 classic horror movie *The Fog)*. Mike and his parents lived in Southwark for three years, then moved to Wimbledon, south-west London, near the famous tennis championships.

Mike was apparently singing Antonio Carlos Jobim's 'Desafinado' in his cot at two years old, around the time that his sister Papita was born. Mike's parents split up when he was five. He started piano and violin at Holly Mount primary, then moved to Raynes Park High School. At fourteen, Mike auditioned for and got into Chetham's, a boarding school in Manchester which specialised in music. He became interested in nature, bird watching, and also started to listen to a lot of music, particularly Bill Withers, The Carpenters, ELP, Stevie Wonder and Genesis. He started a band called LAG.

Mike passed five 'O' Levels and also got an 'A' Level in music. He was becoming a very promising pianist and drummer and started studying percussion at the Guildhall School Of Music in 1977. He met Phil in his second year, after hearing him playing in a practice room and being amazed at his drumming prowess. Mike stuck his head around the door and they became great mates, spending hours listening to Herbie Hancock and Miles Davis at Phil's flat in Clapham, south London. Mike then met Mark for the first time on Oxford Street in summer 1979, impressing him with some newly-bought Billy Cobham drumsticks.

The Brothers Gould: Boon and Phil

Boon was born Rowland Charles Gould (from this point on, he will be referred to as Boon, but his songwriting credit will state 'R. Gould') on 4 March 1955 in Shanklin on the Isle Of Wight. Phil was born on 28 February 1957 in Hong Kong. Boon and Phil had two elder brothers – Paul and John – and one elder sister, Gillian. Their parents were Rowland and Joy – he was a journalist, a CBS News reporter and good friend of famous American newscaster, Walter Cronkite. Joy was a film critic for the Tokyo Press Club. They had initially settled on the Isle Of Wight but then moved to Hong Kong. The boys saw their parents as being quite glamorous – Phil has seen photos of them with Ava Gardner, Cary Grant and Danny Kaye. Soon after Phil's birth, Rowland and Joy separated and she moved the family back to the Isle Of Wight, settling in Shanklin again.

Boon was so-named when a family friend said he was a real 'boon' to the family with his benign, laid-back nature, and the nickname stuck. The family were never particularly well-off, but they always had student lodgers during the summer months to keep money coming in, and Joy also worked full-time throughout Phil and Boon's childhood. The boys attended St. Wilfrid's Catholic primary school in Ventnor, six miles from home. Both took to music, Phil initially picking up the piano and Boon the violin. Their elder brother, Paul, introduced them to The Beatles, The Rolling Stones and Cream.

Later, Boon went to Sandown Grammar, while Phil went to Fairway Secondary Modern. Phil was becoming an avid reader, devouring books by Carlos Castaneda, Isaac Asimov, Arthur Koestler and Hermann Hesse. He started dabbling with the clarinet and trumpet around this time but also started playing the drums, beguiled by the photo of Yes drummer Bill Bruford on the inside cover of their *Fragile* album. Phil was somewhat of a daydreamer at school but also a gifted writer, and usually top of his English class. He started writing poetry and stories at fourteen, and also invested in a perspex drum kit inspired by Billy Cobham's set inside the gatefold sleeve of his *Spectrum* LP.

Boon and Phil's elder brother, John, left the island to join the RAF in 1968, but on his return, he became a DJ and a big musical inspiration to both Phil and Boon. Boon bought his first guitar from John in 1972 and quickly became obsessed with it. Boon and Phil joined their first band Greyflood – a folk-rock unit – in the same year. Phil left school in 1973 and began working as a deckchair attendant whilst eagerly buying the latest Genesis, Gentle Giant and Yes albums. Boon joined his uncle's electronics firm, working on circuit boards.

John left for London and started working for MCA Records while Phil and Boon formed a band called Joe Bear, playing Doobie Brothers and Steely Dan covers around Cowes and Ryde. Phil wrote his first song, 'Who's The Fool?', around this time, very much informed by teenage angst. Joe Bear played at the 1,000-capacity La Babalu in Ryde, later to be a very important venue for Level 42. Guitarist and local music hero John Wheeler then invited Mark King to guest with Joe Bear in 1975, so suddenly the band had two drummers! Phil was blown away by Mark's talent, and the two of them instantly became great mates, with a shared love of music and sci-fi books. But when Joe Bear disbanded, Phil found himself playing dodgy cover versions in various holiday camps on the island. He was a proper hippie at this point, often drumming in his clogs and finding inspiration in players such as Dave Mattacks, Harvey Mason and Andy Newmark. But he was also becoming more musically ambitious and career-minded too. In 1988, looking back at this period, he told *Modern Drummer* magazine: 'I really wanted to be a serious musician and arranger, something like Deodato. Having grown up in the post-*Bitches Brew* era, with The Mahavishnu Orchestra and all the jazz/fusion of the mid-70s, I was infected with a basic seriousness about music.' Phil also confessed that as late as 1980, he still had dreams of being a famous keyboard player rather than a drummer: 'Although I loved drums and percussion, I still had visions of myself onstage behind a grand piano. I wanted to be Keith Jarrett.'

Boon had his first child with girlfriend Sue James in 1976, naming their daughter Chani. A Greenpeace fundraiser during the same year was also the first time Phil, Boon and Mark played together on the same stage, Mark and Boon sharing bass duties. Boon and Phil then went to the Middle East in December 1977 to play in a covers band for three months. In 1978, at the age of 21, Phil moved to London to begin studying piano and percussion at the Royal Academy Of Music. John Gould introduced Phil to Robin Scott, 'de facto' leader of the band M, who invited Phil to work on their debut album at Mountain Studios in Montreux, Switzerland. There Phil met Wally Badarou (see below), saxophonist Gary Barnacle and local resident David Bowie. (Later, Robin would invite Mark, Phil and Wally to work on M's *Official Secrets* album.)

Phil met Mike while he was drumming in a practice room at the Guildhall School. Boon moved to London and got a job at the *Our Price* record shop on Charing Cross Road. He then reunited with Mark, just down the road in Macari's, and they hatched a plan to visit America. They left in June 1979, initially staying in San Francisco. It was a fun but dangerous time, with drag queens, gangs and guns prevalent. Boon and Mark then went to stay with Boon's uncle in Northern California who put them to work as signwriters. Mark returned to London but Boon stayed on in the USA for six months, briefly moving to San Diego with a girlfriend.

Wally Badarou

Though never a full-time Level 42 member, Wally was an absolutely crucial contributor to the band, a master of synthesizer textures and gifted producer, arranger, songwriter and soundtrack composer. Mark, Phil, Boon and Mike called him 'The Sound Merchant'. Wally was born in Paris and had made a considerable name for himself by 1980, becoming a key part of the so-called Compass Point All Stars alongside drummer Sly Dunbar and bassist Robbie Shakespeare, and appearing on classic albums by Grace Jones, Marianne Faithfull, Talking Heads and Joe Cocker. He was also a trusted collaborator and key ideas man for legendary Island Records founder Chris Blackwell, who also signed Wally to the label as a solo artist in the early 1980s.

Wally brought a whole concept of sound to the Level 42 table, playing superb Moog and Prophet-5 synth, programming the Synclavier digital sampler, producing, composing and mixing. He once outlined his approach to the latter in *Making Music* magazine, giving an insight into the band's meticulous arrangements:

It's something I learnt from (Talking Heads/Robert Palmer/Grace Jones producer/mixing engineer) Alex Sadkin, who used to be a good friend of mine, which is to start mixing the very minute you put a note down. The beginning of recording is the beginning of mixing, and as you work on a track, anything that you add should have its proper status straight away. I don't mean that you can't change things later on, but it's about giving things the best sound and the best surroundings from minute one, with the right type of reverb, panning and so on. It's important because a lot of the overall effect of a track comes from cross-modulation between parts. Some parts might sound strange on their own but fantastic in the total mix, so you don't get a good picture if you're not mixing things properly whilst putting them down.

Wally was also seemingly predestined to enjoy Mark's bass-playing, saying, 'Bass has always been my favourite instrument. I like low sounds, and at the beginning of the 70s, I listened a lot to Deep Purple, as well as things like Jimmy Smith and Santana. I remember being really angry with my father when he bought a piano, because I was just getting into organs, Jon Lord and things'. But for all Wally's huge contribution to Level 42's music, sadly he never appeared live with the band in its original incarnation.

1980: The Birth Of The Band

Boon returned to London from California in January 1980. There he joined Mark, who was refurbishing his friend Martin Daley's flat in Walthamstow, north-east London, and they lived together there for six months. There was no heating in the property and they were living on pies and instant mashed potatoes. But there was a soundproofed home studio upstairs, so there were endless jam sessions (during this time Mark demoed 'Hot Water', of which much more in the chapter on *True Colours*), with Phil sometimes joining them and also Paul Fishman from the band Reflex, who later had a UK hit with 'The Politics Of Dancing'.

In February 1980, Phil suggested that they all get together for a Monday night jam with Mike at the Guildhall School. Dominic Miller, a guitarist friend of Mike's, was also invited along. They played some funky grooves and a good time seemed to be had by all, so a further get-together was planned for the following week. Miller didn't turn up for this second rehearsal, so, by default, Boon became the sole guitarist. According to Boon, by the end of their third rehearsal, they had the bare bones of 'Mr Pink', '88' and 'Love Meeting Love', the latter as yet without vocals.

Their first gig as an unnamed band took place at the Guildhall students union in the Barbican complex, central London. They performed a short set, four or five originals, plus a cover of Lee Oskar's 'Haunted House', but the gig was cut short when complaints from the neighbours brought a visit from the police! But things were moving fast for the band now.

Via John Gould, they were introduced to Andy Sojka, a vital figure in the Level 42 story. He ran the All Ears record shop in Harlesden and also had an indie label called Elite Records, best known for releasing Atmosfear's cult disco/funk classic 'Dancing In Outer Space'. His associate, Jerry Pike, also worked at All Ears and designed the Elite logo. Sojka had his ear to the ground in terms of the nascent jazz/funk scene in the UK and was keen to hear John's brothers' band. Robin Scott reportedly paid for a band showcase at Hollywood Studios in East London (Boon recalled that Light Of The World were rehearsing down the corridor). Andy was initially fairly unimpressed, but he liked the 'Love Meeting Love' bassline and groove. When the song had been developed to his liking, the band duly signed to Elite for six months, contractually obliged to deliver two singles and an album.

At this point, Phil called for Wally, who immediately gave Level 42 credibility, creativity and direction. Although Mike was initially a little reticent about adding a second keyboardist, he quickly realised the benefits of involving such an experienced, highly knowledgeable player. The band were up and running. Now they needed a name. Mark liked 88, but then saw that Roxy Music guitarist Phil Manzanera had put together a short-lived project called Rocket 88. So Mark and Boon suggested *42:* the meaning of life in Douglas Adams' book, *The Hitchhiker's Guide To The Galaxy*. 42 was subsequently scribbled down on the Elite contract, but apparently Sojka on a whim suggested adding Level. He quickly sought approval from the band and it was official – Level 42 was born.

The Early Tapes (1980)

Personnel:
Mark King: Bass and Lead Vocals
Mike Lindup: Keyboards and Vocals
Phil Gould: Drums and Percussion
Boon Gould: Guitar and Alto Saxophone
Wally Badarou: Prophet-5 Synthesizer
Leroy Williams: Percussion
Dave Chambers: Tenor and Soprano Saxophone
Producers: Andy Sojka and Jerry Pike for Unbelievable Productions
Engineer: Graham Carmichael
Record Label: Polydor
Recorded: Hillside Studios (London), Gateway Studios (London), March 1980 to August 1980
Released: March 1982
Running Time: 41:44
Highest Chart Placing: UK: 70, US: –
Current edition: 2000 Universal with bonus tracks

Produced by Sojka and Jerry Pike, *The Early Tapes* was recorded in two bursts – during March 1980 at Gateway Studios in Clapham, South London, and the rest during August 1980 at Hillside Studios in Streatham (very near where both Mark and Boon would later own properties). Mike was ideally placed for these sessions, spending most of summer 1980 living with his mum down the road in Wimbledon. Boon and Mark were also nearby, crashing with John Gould at his Balham flat (John told band biographer Michael Cowton that he remembers Mark sitting on his sofa, saying, 'I'm going to be a millionaire by the time I'm 30'!), and they often all took off to rehearse at the Goulds' garage on the Isle Of Wight.

The five songs needed to complete the album were recorded in August 1980 during a frenetic ten-day spurt. They'd work from ten to six, heading to the local park afterwards for a game of football. The music they were making was rough-and-ready funk, with elements of jazz, Latin, rock and soul, very much under the twin influences of Herbie Hancock and Stanley Clarke. The addition of Wally to the sessions was proving to be an absolute masterstroke – as well as being a brilliant keyboard player, he was also a shrewd arranger and indispensable 'extra pair of ears'.

By no means were the band making enough income from their music to live on at this point: Boon was working full-time in a warehouse, seven days a week, ten hours a day. Meanwhile, Polydor had agreed to license two singles ('Love Meeting Love' and 'Flying On The Wings Of Love') from Elite for £8,000. A songwriting deal was also agreed with ATV Publishing, helping the band buy some new equipment including Mark's first Jaydee Supernatural bass, built by John Diggins, and Mike's Fender Rhodes bought from Argents on London's

Denmark Street (still open for business at the time of writing) and previously owned by Brian Bennett of The Shadows.

They carried on gigging wherever they could, including two very important shows (5/6 September 1980) at La Babalu nightclub on the Isle Of Wight, scene of Phil and Boon's Joe Bear gig five years previously. Polydor's Maurice Gallagher was sent down to check them out and he returned to London with very favourable notices – there was now a real buzz around Level 42. December 1980 proved to be a crucial month for the band: after a gig at Flicks in Dartford, Kent, they were signed up by Paul Fenn of the renowned Asgard live booking agency. Then *The Early Tapes* was mixed by Sojka at Playground Studios in Camden Town, north-west London, and also the band celebrated signing a five-album deal with Polydor.

It was to be a happy Christmas. Britfunk was booming, and the band's live diary for 1981 was already getting busy. *The Early Tapes* wouldn't be released by Polydor until March 1982 (early editions bore the inscription 'Level Records', to make it look like an indie/underground release), almost eighteen months after it was recorded, but Sojka had originally intended it to come out in early 1981 with a sleeve design by Atmosfear bassist Lester Bachelor – later scrapped in place of Polydor's reversion, which used artist Joy Barling Loyla's iconic band logo, of which much more soon.

'Sandstorm' (Badarou/King) 4:40

Recorded at Hillside Studios in August 1980 and originally titled 'Shot In The Head', 'Sandstorm' was actually the very first release in the Level 42 catalogue, appearing on the B-side of a twelve-inch promo single on Elite Records whose A-side was 'Journey To' by jazz/funk band Powerline.

Heavily influenced by Herbie Hancock's 'I Thought It Was You', 'Sandstorm' kicks off with Phil's double-tracked, military-style snare drum intro – an original and arresting introduction. Thereafter it really is 'Wally world', a stunning, panoramic display of his synth techniques. The opening section sees Mike play some funky Fender Rhodes in the left channel, Wally his patented Prophet-5 'haunted house' chords in the middle, and Boon and Wally injecting beguiling little countermelodies on the right (and if you listen closely, Wally also adds some more synth stabs on the left channel, first heard at 0:46). There's also more than a hint of 'Hot Water' in Mark's bassline.

At 2:22, Wally cuts in with a great synth break (close listening reveals Mike joining in on Rhodes) and Mark embarks on the first of many memorable sixteenth-note finger-style workouts. Boon's acoustic guitar then features strongly, an original and unexpected touch.

'Sandstorm' is a fine introduction to the band's sound world, showcasing their natural playing and arranging skills. Everyone gets their chance to shine and all the melodic motifs combine to create a funky and memorable piece, played live regularly between 1980 and 1983.

'Love Meeting Love' (King/P. Gould) 6:23

Arguably the most important track in the band's discography, the Level story really started here. It was recorded during March 1980 at Gateway Studios in Clapham. An early instrumental version, with the working title of 'Love Making Love', was the first track to pique Andy Sojka's interest. He was apparently intrigued by the rolling bass vamp, and, sensing the potential of the song, requested that some vocals be added. Mark and Phil quickly came up with a melody and a set of lyrics, and then a demo was recorded with a session singer. Realising that the vocals lacked character, everyone in the band had a go at singing it. Mike was perfectly in tune, but something was missing. Phil and Boon's passes were adequate, but everyone agreed that Mark sounded great. In just six months, he had gone from being a drummer to a bassist and lead vocalist: a testament to his natural musical ability and sheer force of will. 'It's just a case of having to do it', he told *Guitarist* magazine in 1991. He also explained to Andy Peebles during Radio 1's *My Top Ten* programme in 1984 that his vocal performance on 'Love Meeting Love' was very influenced by Ali Campbell on UB40's classic single 'Food For Thought'.

The opening minute was all about Mark's memorable bassline (played on a Hayman Modular) and Mike's soothing Rhodes and piano solo (he also performed the arpeggiated Moog melody during the middle section). Dave Chambers, a British session player who had worked with Mike Westbrook, John Kongos and Annette Peacock, was brought in by Sojka, delivering a memorable tenor sax solo. The net result was a lovely slice of shimmering jazz/funk, perfect for long summer evenings.

Originally rush-released as a limited-edition Elite Records twelve-inch single in April 1980, 'Love Meeting Love' was then reissued by Polydor in August 1980. The track's success was a surprise to everyone; it reached number 61 in the UK singles chart, sold around 60,000 copies, garnered a rave review from the esteemed *Blues & Soul* magazine, and also got a vital endorsement by the so-called Funk Mafia (Robbie Vincent, Chris Hill, Jeff Young, Greg Edwards, Froggy et al), a group of DJs who toured the country and had a large coterie of (mostly) young fans.

Mike remembers hearing 'Love Meeting Love' for the first time on the fabled *Powerplay* show on Radio Luxembourg and also recalls respected DJs Peter Powell and John Peel playing it on BBC Radio 1. It was the beginning of the band's career, and they have a lot to thank Andy Sojka for (he passed away in 2000).

An instrumental mix of the track featuring a longer sax solo, titled 'Instrumental Love', has been added to some CD and streaming versions of *The Early Tapes*. The 2012 *Living It Up* box set features an excellent live performance recorded at the Hammersmith Odeon in 1990. 'Love Meeting Love' also very nearly became the title track of Level 42's debut album in 1981, scrapped when a new collection of material was recorded in the spring and summer of that year.

'Theme To Margaret' (King) 4:00

A great testament to Mark's vision of 'positive funk', this was actually his tribute to a deceased relative, originally written in 1976. He explained the genesis of the tune to *The Herts Adviser* in 2010:

> Margaret Flux was actually my grandmother, bless her. I came up with that tune when she passed away. But actually, it was a great lesson because I couldn't think of anything sad. It was just really 'up', and I was thinking 'Oh God, poor old Gran, this is meant to be an elegy to her life, but this thing's up there and flopping around all over the place!'

Mark's opening slapped bass ushers in another exuberant, fresh funk/disco track, recorded at Hillside in August 1980, with a hint of Stanley Clarke's 'Hot Fun' from his classic 1976 album *School Days*. Producers Sojka and Pike get a terrific drum sound, with a snappy snare and cavernous toms. Wally delivers some typically strong playing with his trademark Prophet 'frequencies' at 0:08, familiar to anyone who knows the Grace Jones track 'Walking In The Rain'. Mark lays down a cracking sixteenth-note groove in the solo section and peppers the tune with Clarke-style power chords. And the fast seven-note lick that closes the track and occasionally appears throughout is also reminiscent of Clarke's bass concept.

Mark's ringing harmonic chord closes out another very exuberant, attractive band performance, pleasingly rough around the edges. At the time of writing, 'Theme To Margaret' has only been performed twice in concert, both times in 1981.

'Autumn (Paradise Is Free)' (King) 4:44

Recorded at Gateway in March 1980, this is a pleasant if hardly essential Latin-tinged jazz/funk number, showing that the band were always exceptionally eclectic in their tastes. Despite its fairly anodyne lyrics and slightly uncertain lead vocal, 'Autumn' is another winning performance.

Boon's acoustic guitar is a lovely touch, present in the right channel throughout, at times reminiscent of Brazilian jazz player Laurindo Almeida. Mark's rather shrill vocals are treated with various studio effects. Mike plays some sparkling Rhodes chords and Phil's groove is novel and propulsive. Boon's sax solo won't win any awards for subtlety but adds some much-needed raunch to the track, with an earthy tone and agreeable lack of pre-meditated licks.

Wally's synth melody, beginning at 4:14, is a subtle and engaging addition, with almost Gil Evans-like chord voicings. In the closing section, we finally get to hear special guest Leroy Williams' congas; he was a highly respected American session percussionist who had also played jazz drums with a number of all-time greats including Sonny Rollins, Stan Getz and Thelonious Monk.

'Autumn (Paradise Is Free)' is a pleasant, if hardly essential ending to the original album's first side. At the time of writing, it has never been performed live.

'(Flying On The) Wings Of Love' (Lindup/R. Gould/P. Gould/King/ Badarou) 6:56

Recorded at Gateway in March 1980 and released as the second single from *The Early Tapes*, '(Flying On The) Wings Of Love' reached number 76 in the UK during December 1980. This led to a disastrous guest performance at the Caister Soul Weekender, run by the aforementioned Funk Mafia DJs, as Mark reminisced to *Q Magazine*'s David Hepworth in 1987:

> I'd bought these leather trousers because I thought that's what pop stars did, and it was in the middle of winter because that's the only time they can borrow the holiday camp. We were given microphones and the pair of us shuffled sideways on stage sort of nervously singing. The thing was that I didn't even sing on that record. So I just kept on smiling and slapping my leg. We must have looked like (1960s 'beat' pop band) The Bachelors.

'Wings Of Love' is another effortlessly uplifting track in the Latin-tinged jazz/funk/disco style that was rapidly becoming the band's trademark. Mike composed the lion's share of the piece, getting contributions when needed. His lead vocals are double-tracked, fairly rough-and-ready, but touching in their artless naiveté. Wally provided the instrumental middle-eight (technically a middle-twelve) in his classic ascending/descending style (see the section on 'Something About You'), and supplied the subsequent cheesy-but-great synth solo. The last two minutes of the track feature a full-on disco breakdown, complete with handclaps and Wally's catchy 'milk bottle' keyboard melody.

A light but memorable piece, '(Flying On The) Wings Of Love' has only rarely been played in concert, most recently in 2010.

'Woman' (Lindup) 4:37

Recorded at Hillside Studios in August 1980, this Mike composition is a classic slice of instrumental jazz/funk. It features a little more improvisatory fire than you'd usually expect from the genre, thanks to Phil and Mark's ferocious fusion stylings, and some ripping soprano sax and conga solos.

Mike's opening acoustic piano solo is tentative at times but provides just the right mellow mood for the tune's first half. Close listening reveals Boon's subtle guitar comping in the right channel. Phil's drums sound fantastic and he delivers a great performance, marshalling the band through various sections and riding the cymbal in the style of jazz/rock greats Chester Thompson and Alex Acuna. Dave Chambers contributes a superb soprano sax solo with a touch of Wayne Shorter's tone and a nice sense of space, eliciting a yelp of encouragement from Mark at 2:46, and Leroy Williams provides a fiery closing conga solo.

Possibly the standout from *The Early Tapes*, 'Woman' is an excellent band performance, probably recorded completely live in the studio apart from a few synth overdubs. At the time of writing, it has only been performed once in concert – in Gillingham, Kent, on 13 March 1981, with Boon's guitar supplying the main theme in place of the soprano sax.

'Mr Pink' (King/Badarou) 5:06

Originally named 'Dr Sphincter Funk'(!), this was based on some of Mark's bass grooves developed during the band's early days rehearsing at the Guildhall School of Music. But 'Mr Pink' has become a live favourite, remaining in the band's set up until the time of writing. Along with 'Love Games' and 'Starchild', it's often the only track played to represent the band's early jazz/funk roots.

Recorded at Hillside in August 1980, it still sounds remarkably lo-fi and original in its way, coming out of the Herbie Hancock school but retaining a very 'British' earthiness. Mark's opening bass salvo is occasionally doubled and agreeably in-your-face. His finger-style part at 0:45 is stylistically very similar to Headhunters bassist Paul Jackson, and Phil also sounds uncannily like drummer Harvey Mason at 0:58.

As the piece progresses, it becomes a fascinating compendium of keyboard textures and motifs. For example, in the 'breakdown' section at 2:00, Wally's synths manoeuvre around Mike's Rhodes in the left channel (Wally also plays some fantastic Herbie-style licks in the last 20 seconds of the tune). Mark's bass feature at 4:06 shows that he was now becoming a serious rival to Louis Johnson, Stanley Clarke and other high-speed slappers from across the pond.

A little overlong but full of arresting licks and tricks, 'Mr Pink' was an exciting blueprint for the band and destined to become a fan favourite.

'88' (King) 5:12

Recorded at Hillside in August 1980, '88' was another signature track and live favourite during the band's early years. Kicking off with some very sketchy vocals – not helped by the surfeit of echo and flanging – '88' gets into its stride with Phil's kick drum/tom-tom combo and Boon's excellent rhythm guitar, both with a lot of tape-echo added. Mark's bassline is pretty irresistible and Wally adds some fine synth lines in the right channel, before soloing more extensively on the Minimoog at 2:17. At 3:27, Boon unleashes his first (raw and a little unreconstructed) electric guitar solo of the album, before Phil delivers a great lick around the kit to close the track at 5:05.

If a bit more time had been taken with the vocals (or they'd been removed completely), this would have been an outstanding track. As it is, '88' remains a key artefact of the band's early jazz/funk period and was always a good springboard for live improvisation between 1980 and 1985.

Extra tracks

'Piano' (Lindup) 2:25

A very rough solo-piano demo recorded during *The Early Tapes* sessions, added to some reissues of the album, the brief instrumental 'Piano' is nevertheless well worth seeking out, demonstrating that Mike was already developing an instantly recognisable touch and sense of melody/harmony.

Level 42 (1981)

Personnel:
Mark King: Bass and Lead Vocals
Mike Lindup: Minimoog, Pianos and Vocals
Phil Gould: Drums, Glockenspiel and Timbales
Boon Gould: Guitar
Wally Badarou: Prophet-5, Korg Polyphonic and Minimoog
Leroy Williams: Congas, Bongos and Percussion
Gary Barnacle: Saxophone
Dave Chambers: Saxophone
Producer: Mike Vernon for Handle Artists
Engineer: Dick Plant
Record Label: Polydor
Recorded: Vineyard (London), Chipping Norton Studios (Chipping Norton), April 1981 to June 1981
Released: August 1981
Running Time: 43:16
Highest Chart Placing: UK: 20, US: –
Current edition: 2000 Universal with bonus tracks

Level 42 began 1981 with an all-dayer at The Lyceum in London, playing alongside Guyanese-British pop legend Eddy Grant and hometown jazz/funk heroes UK Players. It was the beginning of a frenetic series of British live dates throughout February, March and April – the Britfunk scene was taking off all around the country, and the band were somewhat fortunate to have such a receptive, readymade audience.

In February, Polydor bought the band out of its Elite contract for a reported £25,000 and considered releasing *The Early Tapes* as Level 42's official debut album. Instead, they opted to record some new material from scratch, backing the band to come up with eight new compositions – and fast. The proverbial 'safe pair of hands' was urgently needed to assist; Polydor recommended Mike Vernon, house producer at Chipping Norton Studios, situated on the edge of the Cotswolds hills in central England. This was a very exciting development for Mark, very much aware of Vernon's pedigree as collaborator with John Mayall's Bluesbreakers, Eric Clapton, Fleetwood Mac and Focus (Mark was particularly keen on the Dutch prog-rock band's 1971 album *Moving Waves*). But time was of the essence, and as such, no demos were prepared for the songs on *Level 42* – the band went straight into 'record' mode, with Vernon quickly demonstrating his technical and musical mastery, and, according to Mike, also singing some uncredited background vocals.

Recording started with the tracking of 'Turn It On' and 'Love Games' at The Vineyard, south-east London, later owned by star producers and PWL label-owners Stock, Aitken and Waterman. There were lots of reports that the studio was haunted – Phil and Mark watched a pool ball rocket into a pocket of its own accord, and later all 24 tracks went into record without anyone being near the desk. Further recording took place at Chipping Norton, Marcus and Red Bus Studios in London, with Mark now exclusively using Jaydee basses, boasting that he had serial numbers three, four and five of his favoured Supernatural Classics.

No one is quite sure who recommended the artist Joy Barling Loyla to Polydor, but her striking 'princess' image (modelled by her sister Kim) was so iconic that it quickly became the unofficial band logo. This was good news for the band – Mark, Mike, Boon and Phil were all keen not to feature their faces on the front of the album, influenced by their favourite fusion and progressive rock covers.

Released in August 1981, *Level 42* was a solid success, selling around 20,000 copies in the UK right off the bat, making number 20 in the charts and staying in the top 100 for eighteen weeks. It also made number five in the Netherlands and eventually achieved gold status there, the beginning of a Dutch love affair with the band's music. The vocal tracks were seen by the group as 'sweeteners', but the three instrumentals were absolutely their bread and butter – they wanted to be known as great players, not just hitmakers.

The 1981 UK tour started at The Venue in London on 21 August (earning a rave review by Alan Coulthard in *Record Mirror*), ending at The Taverners in Haywards Heath. They were then handed a great opportunity when The Police's manager Miles Copeland approached John Gould and offered the band an eight-date support slot on a European tour (in characteristic fashion, Copeland also secured a support slot for his act, Jools Holland & His Millionaires, on Level's forthcoming headlining tour as a 'quid pro quo'). At this point, the trio comprising Sting on bass/vocals, Andy Summers on guitar and Stewart Copeland on drums were probably the biggest band in the UK, so it was a great coup for Level to do the concerts.

But it wasn't an easy ride. The first gig was in Böblingen, southern Germany. There was no soundcheck and they decided to try and dress the part, with leather trousers, silk shirts and 'rock star' finery. It was a disaster. Boon received a choc ice on top of his head ('Under red lights it looked like he was bleeding, but then he started moving and suddenly he looked like Wilko Johnson, he was firing around the stage, dodging the missiles!', Mark told *Guitarist* magazine in 1991), and a firecracker lodged in Mark's armpit ('I swear to God I thought I'd been shot!'). On the second night of the tour – Sting's birthday – they returned to wearing jeans and t-shirts and the gig was a big improvement. During their final show with The Police, at the Olympic Hall in Munich, there was a splendidly Spinal Tap-esque moment when Mark signed off with 'Goodnight, Heidelberg!'.

A further headlining concert at the Paradiso in Amsterdam saw Mark meet his future wife Pia, a local concert promoter. Back in the UK, a famous gig at the Hammersmith Palais on 22 November 1981 garnered a rave review from Steve Sutherland in *Melody Maker*. That magazine's Paolo Hewitt also became a great friend of the band and occasional drinking pal of Mark's, but he experienced a lot of resistance to Level 42 amongst his contemporaries – a residue of punk's natural suspicion of 'upbeat' music.

Despite the album and tour's success, there was still a degree of instability around Level 42 towards the end of 1981 – Mark and Phil did some work with Gary Barnacle and Ross Middleton's hotly-tipped band Leisure Process, a favourite of legendary CBS A&R man Muff Winwood. Mark almost jumped ship from Level until Polydor Head of A&R Alan Sizer made his presence felt. Then, at the end of 1981, guitar legend Jeff Beck enquired about Mark joining himself and drummer Simon Phillips in a new power trio. Again, at the last minute, he thankfully decided to stick with Mike, Boon and Phil.

December 1981 brought further German, Dutch and Belgian gigs, and Pia moved to England to be with Mark. Then came the news that *Level 42* had sold approximately 60,000 albums in the UK, earning the band a much-cherished silver disc.

'Turn It On' (Badarou/King/P. Gould/R. Gould) 4:36

Apparently 'Turn It On' was always intended as the first track on the album, with the full-length version's famous 'fade-in' intro (Mark's idea) featuring Phil's backwards crash cymbal and five quick blasts of Wally's Prophet-5.

Blessed with Boon's infectious guitar riff (another of Mark's melodies), it was the second single from *Level 42*, reaching a slightly disappointing number 57 in the UK, probably not helped by the lack of a promotional video. The verse and chorus melodies were written by Wally and Mark, excellently sung by the latter, a big improvement on his vocal work from just six months earlier. Boon provided lyric contributions throughout while the post-chorus refrain ('You've hit the top so turn it on') was written by Phil. The song also provided the first chance to hear Mike's stunning falsetto, influenced by George Duke and Earth, Wind & Fire's Philip Bailey.

Phil's simple drum part was augmented by prominent *cabasa*, a Roland sequencer, and some milk and wine bottles too, played with drumsticks by Phil and possibly influenced by Robin Scott's art-school sensibility. Mark's chorus bassline sounds similar to Stanley Clarke's on the track 'Hello Jeff' from his 1975 *Journey To Love* album. Also listen out for Mike's tasty piano comping throughout and Wally's funky Moog solo with added scatting. Wally also adds a catchy, descending countermelody in the second chorus (first heard at 1:35).

With its rubbery bassline, catchy riff, lush mix, complex rhythm track and soulful vocals, 'Turn It On' is a superb album opener, and was many people's introduction to the band. An extended mix appeared on early CD versions of *Level 42*, with a longer intro and various keyboard additions. The streaming edition of the album features a live version of the song, recorded for the BBC's *Sight & Sound* TV/radio broadcast from The Regal in Hitchin on 16 February 1983.

'43' (King) 7:02

Mike Vernon was keen to include a track that demonstrated the band's electrifying live sound, and '43' (originally called '42', according to Mike) was just the ticket. It also demonstrates perfectly what he brought to the table in terms of production and instrument placement, with each motif memorable. Recorded at Chipping Norton Studios, '43' is based on a series of coruscating Mark bass riffs, with a drum/percussion interlude acting as a middle section.

Leroy Williams' tambourine is very high in the mix during the opening section, with Boon's funky riff also prominent. Wally's syncopated Prophet-5 licks are heard on the right, almost playing the role of an extra rhythm guitar. Williams' excellent bongo-playing makes an appearance at 3:04, and then Mike's fine Minimoog solo begins at 3:16 – recorded in the studio control room – and he also contributes some lovely Rhodes phrases throughout (especially at 5:40). The band's strong Brazilian influence emerges during the percussion section – Mike outlines a samba cowbell pattern over Phil's driving bass drum/tom-tom beat. This interlude became an extended feature in concert, often with Mark and Mike moving over to a pair of Rototom kits set up on either side of the stage.

'43' was a live staple throughout the early years of the band, a brilliant showcase for all their strengths, and it also became the theme music for BBC Radio 1's *My Top Ten* programme (Mark appeared as a guest on the show in June 1984, choosing The Stranglers 'European Female', John McLaughlin's 'New York On My Mind', Chaka Khan's 'And The Melody Lingers On', Jimi Hendrix's 'Message Of Love', UB40's 'Food For Thought', Miles Davis' 'Right Off', Return To Forever's 'Space Circus', Siouxsie And The Banshees' 'Happy House', Cream's 'Passing The Time', Jan Hammer's 'One To One' and The Mahavishnu Orchestra's 'Meeting Of The Spirits').

'Why Are You Leaving?' (Lindup/P. Gould) 4:34

The band have many memorable ballads dotted throughout their illustrious catalogue, and here's the first. It could even be categorised as an early example of 'neo-soul' – something that George Benson, Roy Ayers or Stevie Wonder might have come up with (coincidentally, it has a few harmonic devices in common with Stevie's 'That Girl').

Mike came up with the basic chord sequence (Gmin7/B-flat13/E-flat7/A-flat13) and tricky bass vamp. Wally's haunting, fast-descending synth chords emphasise the start of each verse, first heard at 0:20. Close listening reveals not one but two Fender Rhodes comping during the second verse. There's an intriguing modulation at 2:14 before Wally supplies some gorgeous Prophet-5 countermelodies and Dave Chambers features strongly on tenor saxophone.

Phil's lyrics are a very direct expression of hurt and abandonment: something of a trait when it comes to the band's 'romantic' material, and a factor maybe sometimes surprising or even shocking to American listeners.

Despite being a fan favourite, 'Why Are You Leaving?' has only been played twice in concert, possibly due to the difficulty of Mark singing lead over such an intricate bass vamp. A 2002 live version is currently available as an extra track on streaming editions of *Level 42*.

'Almost There' (King/P. Gould/R. Gould) 5:43

'Almost There' is the first official document of an almost criminally-tight band: a cracking ensemble performance designed to show off everyone's strengths. It's almost like a funky version of The Mahavishnu Orchestra.

Boon's underrated, super-tight rhythm guitar gets another great workout here. Amongst the opening hi-hats and cowbells, at 0:06 we hear one of Mark's bass trademarks borrowed from Stanley Clarke's box of tricks: a D harmonic bent up to an E.

The track explodes to life with Mike's percussive Rhodes and some stuttering sixteenth notes from Wally's Prophet-5. The main riff is reminiscent of Candido's 1979 cult jazz/funk/disco track 'Jingo'. Mark's vocals sound a little strained, right at the top of his range, with a large Ali Campbell influence again during the refrain beginning at 1:40 (Phil and Mike sing backup during the chorus). A strong Mahavishnu influence emerges when Boon and Mike trade solos. Then Mike doubles Boon's ingenious lead guitar line and Wally's ominous synth tone kicks in at 3:47, gradually escalating in pitch and intensity.

A seriously impressive statement of intent, 'Almost There' was a live favourite during the first five years of the band, often a concert-opener between 1983 and 1985.

'Heathrow' (Badarou) 4:42

The band's second classic instrumental is the only Level 42 track completely written by Wally. According to Mike, 'Heathrow' was named after the London airport because Wally was constantly travelling on planes during this period, and if he ever played a bum note, the band would jokingly threaten him with the sack – which meant yet another trip to Heathrow ...

It features Wally on Hammond organ, Prophet-5 and Moog, and Mike on Fender Rhodes. Wally's panoramic, ominous Moog bassline shudders into life while Phil sets up a shuffle groove in the style of Stanley Clarke's 'Lopsy Lu'. But he finds a novel way to modify Tony Williams' groove from that Clarke track, with an intrepid use of 'ghost notes'. Gary Barnacle's gutsy electric sax solo, embellished with a rack-unit phaser, is reminiscent of Michael Brecker's playing on Steve Khan's 'Some Punk Funk', and Wally comps superbly on Prophet-5 and Hammond. Also listen out for a great moment at 3:22 when Mark mistakenly moves down to an F one bar too early, but the accident sounded so good that it stayed in.

Another early live favourite, 'Heathrow' often opened their sets between 1981 and 1983, sometimes preceded by loud aircraft noises. Demonstrating their love of classic jazz/rock, the band also occasionally quoted from Miles Davis's 'Right Off' during the piece. In October 2012, Boon made his last ever live appearance with Level 42, playing a typically freewheeling solo on 'Heathrow' during their Bristol Colston Hall gig. Phil, Mike and Wally also played it at London's 606 Club on 11 January 2016 (both available to watch on YouTube). The streaming edition of *Level 42* features a fine live version, recorded for the BBC's *Sight & Sound* in February 1983.

'Love Games' (King/P. Gould) 5:13

Many people's first exposure to the band, this was the lead-off single from *Level 42*, reaching number 38 in the UK during April 1981 and also making the top five in Holland and Germany. Polydor were apparently surprised and thrilled by the success of 'Love Games'. Head of A&R Alan Sizer told band biographer Michael Cowton, with admirable restraint: 'The first glimmerings started to appear that the band might actually be doing something'!

In 2018, Mark told Jazz FM's Nigel Williams that his bassline was inspired by US session great Abraham Laboriel's playing on Herb Alpert's 1979 single 'Rise'. The famous synth motif (first heard at 0:16) was composed by Mark and played by Wally on a Prophet-5. Wally also performs the famous synth/scat solo, not Mike, though the latter was quick to learn it and play it note-for-note in concert.

Both *Blues & Soul* and *Melody Maker* gave 'Love Games' rave reviews, but the *NME* were not so keen. No official video was made for the song, but Level made their *Top Of The Pops* debut with it on 23 April 1981. The band also mimed to the track during their cameo in a little-known 1986 British movie *The Fantasist*, filmed in Dublin and starring Christopher Cazenove and Timothy Bottoms, available to watch on YouTube.

'Love Games' has become one of the band's signature pieces and a live favourite too. A longer mix, featuring some extended sections and a brief acoustic piano solo by Mike, appeared on the first CD version of *Level 42* and is currently available on the streaming edition of the album, alongside an excellent 1983 BBC live version.

'Dune Tune' (King) 4:50

'Dune Tune' is one of Mike's all-time Level 42 favourites, and is also cited by Wally (during an August 2014 interview with *Classic Pop* magazine) as one of his two favourites, the other being 'Something About You'.

Mark's classic bass-led instrumental is a kind of a homage to Stanley Clarke's 'Desert Song' (alluded to in the title) from the classic 1976 album *School Days*. It might also reference Frank Herbert's 1965 science fiction novel, a favourite of Mark and Phil's. Mark's melody uses open strings (E, A and D) as a counterpoint, also a Clarke trademark. The piece explodes into life at 1:46 with Mark's prowling bassline, Leroy Williams' congas (heard in the left channel) and *cabasa*, Mike's exotic Fender Rhodes and Wally's spacey synths. According to Mike, the wordless vocals (first heard at 3:01) accompanying Mark's final melody line were inspired by Airto Moreira's work with Miles Davis on tunes such as 'Selim'. The final section features Wally's brilliant violin-like synth solo, performed on a Prophet-5.

Taken as a whole, the piece is a remarkably assured bass performance and composition from someone who'd barely been playing the instrument for eighteen months. 'Dune Tune' was a live favourite throughout the early years of the band, and also became a regular part of Mark's solo bass improvisations. A *Sight & Sound* live recording from 1983 is available on streaming editions of *Level 42* and has also occasionally been added to CD reissues.

'Starchild' (Badarou/P. Gould/King) 6:02

The third single from *Level 42*, released in November 1981 and reaching number 47 in the UK, 'Starchild' started life as an instrumental by Wally, featuring the famous bass riff and syncopated synth chords. He played it to the rest of the band during rehearsals for *The Early Tapes*. Phil worked hard on it, coming up with the melody and a full set of lyrics very influenced by his love of sci-fi movies, especially Stanley Kubrick's *2001: A Space Odyssey*.

Phil starts the track unaccompanied on a set of Rototoms augmenting his regular kit, before settling into a groove featuring a disco hi-hat pattern, a rarity in the Level catalogue. But the song is essentially a vehicle for Wally's ingenious synth layering, with three distinct motifs distinguishable during the first verse. The instrumental section (kicking off at 3:04) features Phil on glockenspiel and Mike on grand piano doubling a very attractive, intricate melody – they recorded it together at RAK Studios in North London during the final sessions for the album.

Blessed with some striking Joy Barling Loyla cover artwork, 'Starchild' became a favourite of club DJs in New York City such as future Madonna collaborator John 'Jellybean' Benitez, and was frequently heard at nightspots like The Loft and The Funhouse. Level were one of the few British acts who made an impression in the States during the post-punk era, the others being The Slits, Cabaret Voltaire, The Specials, PiL, A Certain Ratio, Joy Division, The Clash, Central Line, Ian Dury, Depeche Mode, Eddy Grant, Blancmange, Heaven 17 and Yazoo.

According to Mike, 'Starchild' is the one Level 42 song always performed at soundchecks, as it perfectly demonstrates the band's instrumental and vocal palette. An extended mix with a much longer instrumental outro was included on early editions of the *Level 42* CD and is also currently available on streaming platforms.

Extra tracks
'Forty Two' (King/P. Gould/R. Gould/Lindup) 6:37

The B-side to 'Love Games', this is one of the band's key early instrumentals. It's a total group composition, a complex piece with a variety of grooves and flavours, recorded live at London's RAK Studios during the final sessions for *Level 42*.

The first section features Mike's infectious Moog melody, some great Afro-funk guitar from Boon and sundry percussion instruments from Leroy Williams including shaker, *cabasa*, congas and cowbell. At 3:18 there's a terrific bass/Moog 'duel' between Mark and Mike, before Mark audibly cues the rest of the band (at 5:57) for the powerful finale.

'Forty Two' is an uplifting piece with some excellent performances. Well worth seeking out, it's available on streaming versions of *Level 42* and the 2000 two-CD reissue.

'Beezer One' (P. Gould/R. Gould/King/Lindup/Badarou) 7:09

A real diversion for the band, this extended blues/R&B curio is essentially just an overlong studio jam session, sounding very much like a contractual obligation. Originally appearing on the B-side of the 'Turn It On' twelve-inch single, it's only really notable for Mark's hyperactive scat intro, one of Boon's longer guitar solos and some fairly decent tenor-playing from Dave Chambers. 'Beezer One' appears on the streaming version of *Level 42*.

'Foundation And Empire Parts 1 and 2' (King) 8:26

Named after Isaac Asimov's 1952 science fiction novel, this epic 'Starchild' B-side was a fine attempt to approach the kind of cosmic jazz/rock made famous in the mid-1970s by artists such as Stanley Clarke, George Duke and Chick Corea's Return To Forever. There are a myriad of treats on offer, most notably Mark's deft playing throughout, and Mike's terrific Fender Rhodes and Moog. An ambitious and largely successful undertaking, 'Foundation And Empire' is currently available on the streaming version of *Level 42* and the 2000 two-CD reissue.

'Goodbye Ray Schmidt-Volk' (King/Lindup/P. Gould/R. Gould) 2:07

A brief but amusing track, recorded and mixed very quickly, and only discovered on a cassette circa 2001, this was a goodbye present for a particularly important employee of Polydor Records in Germany. Mark first bids farewell to Ray in a deep 'DJ' voice, before breaking into some old-school rapping in the style of Melle Mel (to no one's great surprise, he's an absolute natural). Clocking in at barely two minutes long, 'Goodbye Ray Schmidt-Volk' is actually one of the band's more potent grooves, currently available on streaming versions of *Level 42* and the 2000 two-CD reissue.

The Pursuit Of Accidents (1982)

Personnel:
Mark King: Vocals, Bass, Keyboard Additions and Percussion
Mike Lindup: Vocals, Prophet-5, Minimoog, Acoustic/Electric Pianos and Percussion
Phil Gould: Drums, Percussion, Roland Rhythm Composer and Backing Vocals
Boon Gould: Guitars
Wally Badarou: Prophet-5 and Solina String Ensemble
Pete Wingfield: Clavinet
Pete Jacobsen: Jupiter 4
Producer: Mike Vernon
Engineers: Jerry Boys, Dave Bascombe, Gordon Milne
Record Label: Polydor
Recorded: Eden (London), Battery (London), Vineyard (London), Chipping
Norton (Chipping Norton), Red Bus (London), Maison Rouge (London), February
1982 to June 1982
Released: September 1982
Running Time: 45:05
Highest Chart Placing: UK: 17, US: –
Current edition: 2000 Universal with bonus tracks

At the outset of 1982, though the band were pleased with the reaction to
their debut album, all in the Level 42 garden was not completely rosy. They
were gaining more and more traction in the live sphere, but the pressure
was on. Polydor wanted the band to keep progressing – record-company-
speak for 'have some more hits' – but Phil, in particular, was determined to
maintain their credibility as top-notch instrumentalists. Besides, there was a
lot of pressure on him to provide lyrics to order. He was rapidly becoming
the 'conscience' of the band, a role he took seriously and one from which he
derived great pride, but it also took its toll.

The March release of *The Early Tapes* briefly gave some pause for thought,
but as planning for the new album began, the band were now keen to take
more control and produce themselves. Songs were also urgently needed, but
they were confident they could deliver the goods in the studio. Early sessions
at Eden in London, with assistance from up-and-coming producer/engineer
Nick Launay were fairly fruitless but did spawn a rough version of 'Are You
Hearing (What I Hear)?' and the basic tracks for 'The Pursuit Of Accidents'.
Sizer and Polydor were not happy with this scant return. The band eventually
had to eat humble pie and realise the experiment hadn't worked.

Mike Vernon was called in again to salvage a tricky situation. The band then
spent ten days writing and recording at Maison Rouge Studios before heading off
for another European and UK tour during April and May 1982, including debut
gigs at London's legendary Hammersmith Odeon. But a poorly-attended show at
The Limit in Sheffield led to a fractious meeting with manager John Gould and
Sizer; the latter was now keen for Mark to take more of a lead in the band.

There was a rush to complete *The Pursuit Of Accidents* (a title close to something J. G. Ballard or David Bowie might have come up with: Bowie's *Low* had two working names, one of which was *Planned Accidents*) in June and July, with sessions split between Chipping Norton, Marcus, Eden, Vineyard, Red Bus, Basing Street and Battery studios. 'The Chinese Way' was the last song recorded for the album, with Phil reportedly having just two hours to deliver his lyrics.

But there was plenty more going on during the summer of 1982: Mark married Pia on the Isle Of Wight, and he also discovered a sub-clause in his Polydor contract calling for solo material. He got together with Mike to record a one-off twelve-inch single called 'Freedom', credited to Thunderthumbs And The Toetsenman. It was released on 9 July but didn't chart.

Pursuit was finally released in September. Anecdotally, it seems to be many American fans' favourite Level album, though apparently was not rated particularly highly by Mark, Mike, Phil and Boon. It's a fascinating, transitional collection, in that you can sense them feeling their way towards being a 'song' band, whilst not wanting to alienate their hardcore following. Lyrically, *Pursuit* is darker than *Level 42*, and the general sound is much 'edgier', less lush, much more akin to their live approach, foregrounding Phil's whip-crack snare and four-on-the-floor grooves. Mike Vernon also took a lot more time with Mark's much-improved vocals this time around, with frequent double-tracking and some intricate arrangement ideas. All in all, *Pursuit* is an excellent consolidation and effective distillation of the classic Level sound.

The gorgeous cover art by Joy Barling Loyla was a striking extension of her *Level 42* design concept, though no one was very happy with Jay Myrdal's group portrait. As Mike told biographer Michael Cowton, 'There was a horrible photograph on the back, with us sort of smoking. They didn't use smoke, though; it was a type of incense – tons of it'.

Paolo Hewitt gave *Pursuit* a rave review in *Melody Maker*, but otherwise, the critical reception was rather mixed, though it found its way to number 17 in the UK charts. Mark and Pia celebrated the birth of their first daughter Florrie in October 1982, during a lengthy UK and European tour which climaxed with another gig at the Hammersmith Odeon on 7 November.

'Weave Your Spell' (Lindup/P. Gould/King) 5:30

Stylistically, 'Weave Your Spell' carries on where 'Starchild' left off, but there's a distinctly 'spikier' mix – cleaner, brighter snare/cymbals and heavier, 'gated' tom-toms. Mark's bass sound has a lot more presence, with a touch of slapback echo too. Mike's vocals have developed a great deal since the debut album, sounding fuller and richer, and he also takes the lead instrumentally with a fine acoustic piano solo at 1:58.

A fusion of funk, disco and Latin elements, the song doesn't sound like much else on *Pursuit*, and its fairly static F-sharp tonal centre gets a little trying. The percussion section – beginning at 4:10 – also seems surplus to requirements. Released in October 1982 as the second single from the album, 'Weave Your

Spell' reached 43 in the UK. Larry Alexander completed an extended remix for the American market, but it failed to chart there. A video was also made for the song, a fairly undignified affair directed by David G. Hillier, featuring a blank-faced, white-suited Mike strolling around a restaurant – actually it looks more like a studio set from a dodgy 1980s sitcom – before literally being caught in his paramour's 'web' during the piano solo.

At the time of writing, 'Weave Your Spell' has only been played once in concert, in Rotterdam on 19 October 1982, possibly a clue as to the band's opinion of the song.

'The Pursuit Of Accidents' (Badarou/King/Lindup/P. Gould) 7:43

The epic instrumental title track was edited down from an improvised twenty-minute jam, taped at Eden Studios by Nick Launay. Mark's raucous count-in emphasises the natural exuberance and camaraderie of this band in full flight, whether in studio or onstage.

Wally later overdubbed a synth melody (first heard at 0:45) and various other keyboard parts, including a great funky 'rhythm guitar' section at 3:31 and freewheeling Moog solo at 5:58. There are several percussion overdubs (check out some great cowbell work in the right channel, starting at 2:28). Mike has spoken of his pride in his fine Fender Rhodes solo at 4:10, performed live during the tracking session and very reminiscent of jazz/funk legend Lonnie Liston Smith.

Boon also plays a brief but impressive guitar solo at 5:32, with a much creamier, more distorted sound than usual – it sounds like he had invested in some new outboard equipment since the debut album. A Stewart Copeland influence is possibly discernible in Phil's playing, his snare flams and fills reminiscent of The Police sticksman's work on tracks like 'Voices Inside My Head' and 'When The World Is Running Down (You Make The Best Of What's Still Around)'.

All in all, 'The Pursuit Of Accidents' is a vibrant, arresting piece of work, and it joined the fast-growing list of classic instrumentals from the band. A live version, taken from the BBC's *Sight & Sound Live* broadcast of February 1983, appears on streaming editions of the album.

'Last Chance' (P. Gould/King/Lindup) 4:30

A neat bit of sequencing makes the opening of 'Last Chance' sound like a 'happy' continuation of the previous title track – it's virtually identical in tempo and shares the same key. In fact, it's not hard to fathom that 'Last Chance' might have at one point been mooted for a single, featuring as it does a cool verse groove and catchy chorus featuring Mike's vocals at their most beatific (also listen out for his percussive Fender Rhodes in the right channel during the last verse, beginning at 2:54).

Guest synth player Pete Jacobsen (a blind English keyboardist who had worked with British jazz legends Barbara Thompson and Morrissey-Mullen) is audible during the opening eight bars, playing the little bell-like sound in the left channel, and he also contributes a soaring solo beginning at 2:23. 'Last Chance' is the first really exciting finger-style bass workout in Mark's discography. It's arguably his best vocal thus far too, with great diction and character. It's clear that he was becoming a really good singer by this point.

A minor but enjoyable track, at the time of writing 'Last Chance' has only been played live once (at Mainz, Germany, on 14 February 1983) presumably due to the challenging nature of the bassline and its attendant vocal melody. An extended mix has also emerged on YouTube, with extended instrumental sections, an *a cappella* interlude, more lead guitar and a second synth solo by Jacobsen.

'Are You Hearing (What I Hear)?' (King/P. Gould/R. Gould) 4:58

This was the first track recorded for *Pursuit* and the album's lead-off single, released during April 1982 and reaching a disappointing number 49 in the UK charts. It got some airplay from Terry Wogan on BBC Radio 2 though, but he called the band 'Junction 42'!

In the opening 30 seconds, Wally puts together a subtle 'potpourri' of interlocking synth licks, crossing the stereo spectrum, while Mark and Boon play a brilliantly logical, ascending lick, starting in F#. Mark's fine lead vocal is double-tracked throughout the song. Guest clavinet player Pete Wingfield (who had a big 1975 hit on both sides of the Atlantic with 'Eighteen With A Bullet' and also produced Dexys Midnight Runners' *Searching For The Young Soul Rebels*) can be heard 'answering' Mark's vocal lines during the chorus, first audible at 0:43.

The second verse ups the ante, with Boon and Wally exchanging little motifs in the left and right channels alongside Mark's vocals. At 2:23, Mark indulges in some amusing scatting in place of a third verse, possibly a symptom of the pressure Phil was under to provide lyrics. There's then a rather superfluous Samba-tinged percussion blowout in the middle, with Phil and Mark manning the Rototoms, timbales and cowbells – a section often extended when the band played the song live, with Mike also often taking over on the drum kit.

'Are You Hearing (What I Hear)?' is a really strong single and one of the band's best. The twelve-inch remix featured more synths in the breakdowns, more punch on Mark's bass and some chorus effects on his vocals. A live version, taken from the BBC's 1983 *Sight & Sound* broadcast, appears on streaming editions of *Pursuit*.

'You Can't Blame Louis' (King/P. Gould/Badarou) 5:06

Kicking off side two of the original album, 'You Can't Blame Louis' is a real sonic standout, with a bright, clear, nuanced mix. Phil's hi-hat work is intricate from the get-go and his snare drum is snappy and crisp. It's good to hear Mark's bass without any chorus effects added, unadorned and funky, and his soulful vocals are double-tracked in the style of UB40's Ali Campbell (and listen out for his amusing ad-libs during the fade). Mike contributes some lush, creamy Fender Rhodes chords, while Boon delivers a typically memorable acoustic guitar solo at 3:01, doubled by Phil's glockenspiel in the second half.

Lyrically, the song is a classic Phil story about the loss of innocence – a likeable but somewhat wet-behind-the-ears young man finds his idealism tested when a love affair in the big city doesn't turn out quite as he planned it.

Somewhat of a forgotten gem, 'You Can't Blame Louis' was briefly mooted as the second single from *Pursuit*, in the end usurped by 'Weave Your Spell'. It has only been played twice in concert, in 2001 and 2002, the latter performance being included as an extra track on the streaming version of the album.

'Eyes Waterfalling (The Prodigy)' (King/P. Gould/Lindup/Boon) 5:59

It's not every day you hear a 'pop' song that begins with an Art Blakey-style, snare-drum press roll. But that's what we get from Phil on this fan favourite. The track begins with an atmospheric, rubato jam session featuring some great volume-pedal work from Boon, sparkling Rhodes chords from Mike, and judicious use of chorus and delay from Mark. Mike Vernon introduces a great 'explosion' effect at 0:48, bouncing across the stereo spectrum.

Then the groove starts in earnest, and what a groove: Mark lays down a sprightly, slapped bassline, and the song's basic C-min7/D-min7/A-min7/B-min7 chord progression again suggests a possible Police influence. Mark's lead vocal is particularly strong, if at times a little shrill, and there's an intriguing instrumental section at 4:05 featuring tack piano (or dulcimer?) and a very novel 'milk bottle' synth sound. The final section starting at 5:17 highlights Boon's ingenious artificial harmonics and a gorgeous, soft, double-tracked falsetto vocal from Mike. His eerie, suspended B-flat/F Fender Rhodes chord concludes a fine track, possibly their most ambitious yet, played regularly in concert between 1982 and 1985.

Phil's heartfelt lyric was inspired by *Beneath The Wheel*, a 1906 book by German-Swiss poet and novelist Hermann Hesse, reissued in 1957 as *The Prodigy*. It's the story of a gifted child who wins a place at a privileged education establishment. He is sent away to the school by his rather demanding parents, but his disillusionment and loneliness precipitate a serious mental illness. He returns to his home village and finds that he can't reassimilate into society, and is later found drowned. Mark rather unsubtly introduced the 1983 BBC *Sight & Sound* live version as a song 'about a little boy who can't cope with life and does himself in', available to hear on streaming editions of *Pursuit*.

'Shapeshifter' (King) 5:09

This album's 'Dune Tune', 'Shapeshifter' is a fine Mark instrumental with lots of good ideas, intriguing textures and arresting sections. Phil's use of a drum machine foreshadows some of the band's later rhythm experiments, as does

Wally's sequencer that introduces the piece. Wally also adds a new colour to his palette, a Solina string synth which kicks in for the first time at 1:14.

Mark's bass performance is beautifully realised, and Wally's Moog melody at 1:22 and subsequent solo are real earworms. Phil's acoustic drums return at 3:20 and 'Shapeshifter' becomes a buoyant little tune, with Boon's delay-drenched guitar and Mike's almost Caribbean-sounding synth motif taking centre stage. Wally supplies a faintly ominous horror-movie fadeout (perhaps giving rise to the song's title) on his Solina, a perfect closing touch as the track fades away into the night.

Incongruously heard as background music in Les Blair's cult British 1986 film (and Richard E. Grant's screen debut) *Honest, Decent And True*, 'Shapeshifter' has never been played live at the time of writing but remains one of the most intriguing instrumentals in the band's catalogue.

'The Chinese Way' (King/P. Gould/Badarou) 5:54

A great bit of album sequencing, bursting out of the speakers after the low-key 'Shapeshifter', 'The Chinese Way' was the only hit single from *Pursuit* and another last-minute 'bacon-saving song', as Phil was fond of calling them.

Originally based on a Wally demo, 'The Chinese Way' tapped into the UK fashion for all things oriental during 1982, typified by the pop success of the David Sylvian-fronted group Japan and Ridley Scott's movie *Blade Runner*. It was suddenly very cool to wear a t-shirt with obscure Chinese lettering on the front, as indeed Mark did when performing the song on *Top Of The Pops*.

'The Chinese Way' came together in a piecemeal fashion: Wally found himself singing 'The Chinese space disco' over his syncopated synth riff. This gave Phil a direction for his lyric, though he apparently only had a few hours to come up with the words and remains slightly embarrassed by them to this day. His main gripe is that Mandarin is the main language of China, not Cantonese. But, to be fair, elsewhere he comes up with some evocative, subtle lines ('Words of wisdom from the dragon days'). Mark added his wicked bassline and Phil kicked in with a crisp, four-on-the-floor groove, and suddenly they had something fantastic going. Mike chimed in with a superb synth solo at 2:34, and Wally supplied a lovely 'chord cloud' across the stereo spectrum at 3:01.

The song is also helped along by some top-notch recording and engineering work – Phil's bass drum positively explodes from the speakers. But 'The Chinese Way' is also a decidedly odd pop hit, its bizarre song structure possibly reflecting the speed in which it was conceived and recorded: the first 'middle eight' appears after the first chorus, and then the second chorus doesn't appear until the very end of the song.

Released as the third single from *Pursuit* on 7 January 1983, and graced with some striking cover artwork by Alan Brooks, 'The Chinese Way' reached number 24 in the UK charts (but surely would have gone higher had it been the first single), spawned two *Top Of The Pops* appearances and made a lot of new fans (including this one) in the process. The track also gave their live shows a new impetus and energy, and it's a regular concert-closer to this day.

Extra tracks

'It's A Happening' (King/Lindup/P. Gould/R. Gould) 4:54

This is a very strange R&B jam that sounds like it was recorded live in the studio after a few beverages were consumed, complete with fake crowd noises. It was actually the first thing laid down for *Standing In The Light*, produced by Nick Launay at Eden during February 1983.

'The Return Of The Handsome Rugged Man' (P. Gould/King) 5:58

Arguably the band's greatest ever instrumental, this B-side to the twelve-inch version of 'Are You Hearing (What I Hear)?' is an extended jazz/rock/funk jam and a great distillation of the band's fusion influences. But their voice comes through loud and clear, with Phil and Mark's sense of groove and natural instrumental prowess instantly recognisable. Boon's guitar solo is possibly his finest on record, and Mike's Rhodes comping is tasty and exciting.

Standing In The Light (1983)

Personnel:
Mark King: Vocals, Bass and Rototoms
Mike Lindup: Vocals, Prophet-5, Memory Moog, Acoustic/Electric Pianos and Vocoder
Phil Gould: Drums, Backing Vocals, Rototoms, Marimba and Milk Bottles
Boon Gould: Guitars
Wally Badarou: Prophet-5 and Emulator
Paulinho Da Costa: Percussion
Andrew Woodfolk: Soprano Saxophone
Producers: Wally Badarou, Larry Dunn and Verdine White
Engineers: Chris Brunt, Barbara Rooney and Paul O'Duffy
Record Label: Polydor (UK/Europe), A&M (USA)
Recorded: Marcus Studios (London), The Complex (Los Angeles), March 1983 to May 1983
Released: 19 August 1983
Running Time: 40:59
Highest Chart Placing: UK: 9, US: –
Current edition: 2000 Universal with bonus tracks

1983 began with the release of the 'The Chinese Way' single and then a gig at London's Brixton Ace (now the Brixton Academy) on 3 February, supported by The Flying Pickets. There were also tentative steps towards recording a new album; a few early sessions took place at London's Marcus Studios with Wally in the producer's chair and Paul Staveley O'Duffy (Amy Winehouse, Swing Out Sister) engineering. But then came the exciting news that two members of the huge-selling American band Earth, Wind & Fire were interested in working with Level 42. Bassist Verdine White (brother of singer/songwriter/producer Maurice) and keyboard player Larry Dunn had become fans while touring the UK in 1982, both apparently very taken with 'Starchild'.

On the face of it, it was a perfect match; Level had always been inspired by Black American music, and the second invasion of British pop bands was well underway in the States (an extraordinary chart from mid-July 1983 showed 20 of the top 40 US singles being by UK artists, including seven of the top ten), potentially giving Mark, Phil, Mike and Boon a route into that market. The approach from Verdine and Larry was also great timing – Wally was as vital to Level 42 as ever but was also being asked by Island Records to limit the work he was doing outside his solo career.

There were a few hiccups during *Standing*'s pre-production period: Verdine was apparently none too impressed when he flew over to the UK six weeks before the start of recording to hear what the band had been working on, and was played just three new bass riffs. So, as usual, a lot of material would have to be worked up in the studio, and there was the ever-present pressure to produce hits, resting mainly on Mark and Phil's shoulders (Boon took a back seat on *Standing*, not contributing any lyrics), though Phil's heart lay in the darker, more personal material like 'I Want Eyes' and 'The Machine Stops'.

Nevertheless, Polydor's initial panic about a lack of songs led them to recommend 'outside' writers for the first time in the band's career, such as Allee Willis and Bernard 'Beloyd' Taylor, both of whom had co-written several Earth, Wind & Fire classics (Willis co-composed 'September' and 'Boogie Wonderland', Taylor co-penned 'Getaway' and 'You Are A Winner'). Generally, Verdine and Larry would be on the band's side during negotiations with the label, protecting them from the 'conveyer belt' Los Angeles pop machinery and encouraging them to be themselves.

The *Standing* album sessions proper started in early spring 1983. They recorded at The Complex – Maurice White's studio – and were joined by two esteemed guest musicians: first-call percussionist Paulinho Da Costa, who had recently played on Michael Jackson's *Thriller*, and regular Earth, Wind & Fire saxophonist Andrew Woodfolk. There was no question about it – this was the real deal. Phil was particularly thrilled to be amongst the cream of the L.A. session elite. It was a dream come true. Quincy Jones and Stevie Wonder dropped by to say hello, and Phil remembers bumping into Louis Johnson and George Duke in the car park, both working on Duke's album, *Guardian Of The Light*.

Mark, Mike, Phil and Boon took up residence at The Marina, a pleasant apartment block near Venice Beach. After a morning swim and healthy breakfast, recording would generally start at 2 pm and go on until around 11 pm. They never worked at weekends, so there was lots of downtime. One night, after a party hosted by Larry, Mark floored his rented Mercury Capri on Interstate 405 towards San Diego. Hauled over by the cops, he initially tried to fob them off by summoning his 'poshest' British accent, but it didn't work – he had to spend a very unpleasant night in jail, and was later bailed out by Verdine and Larry.

There were some initial communication problems in the studio, with Mike's very proper pronunciation apparently causing much mirth among the American contingent (particularly his rendering of 'in the middle'). But Larry and Verdine were 'hilarious', according to Phil: family guys with a strong work ethic. They were also musically very shrewd, dialling down the rock influences and dialling up the funk and soul, eschewing horns and strings to differentiate Level 42 from Earth, Wind & Fire and other R&B acts of the era. Even on *Standing*'s heavier moments, the music always had a light touch, with lots of space to breathe. The back-room staff at The Complex were also highly skilled and very popular with the band, Mark particularly heralding the work of engineer Chris Brunt.

In May, Level interrupted recording to play their first stateside concert at New York City's Bottom Line for the *Britain Salutes New York* festival, with Stevie Wonder, George Duke and Lenny White in attendance. By all accounts the gig went very well, but it still seemed that no one was quite sure how to promote the band in the US. They were still playing wherever they could, and still packing up their own gear. Polydor International press and promotion manager Sara Silver wanted them to do more press conferences, feeling that American audiences would take to the band more if they got to know them as individuals. Experienced tour coordinator Paul Crockford was brought in to help maximise their live potential, later of course to become a very important figure in the Level story.

In July 1983, they made their auspicious debut at the *Montreux Jazz Festival* (Mark later receiving a very appreciative letter from legendary festival MD Claude Nobs) and *Standing* was finally released on 19 August. It was a solid success, reaching number 9 in the UK and eventually achieving gold status worldwide. It had been a long, strange trip, but a great learning experience which they would never forget. Though the plan had been to break Level 42 in America, they would have to wait another three years for major success – *Standing* didn't chart in the USA and was only released there as part of a one-off deal with A&M Records.

But the band's live following in the UK and Europe was steadily growing, as was their confidence that they could always deliver the goods in concert. They had plenty of practice: they were essentially on the road from 29 August 1983 until the end of the year. Their spellbinding Brixton Ace gig on 25 November was filmed and later broadcast as part of the BBC's *Whistle Test On The Road* TV programme.

'Micro Kid' (Badarou/King/P. Gould/Bernard 'Beloyd' Taylor/Allee Willis) 4:45

Issued as the third single from the album (and with a working title of 'Snakes And Ladders'), 'Micro Kid' was released in October 1983 and reached UK number 37, probably a fair position for a middling Level song (a video was also made, but is very hard to find these days). The track also featured two 'outside' writers, apparently foisted on the band by Polydor: Allee Willis was a hugely respected figure, while Bernard 'Beloyd' Taylor became a great mentor and confidante for Phil.

But 'Micro Kid' makes for a decent album opener – a light, funky tune with drop-D tuning from Mark and lots of memorable licks and motifs. Weirdly, Mark claims (in the liner notes to the *Very Best Of Level 42* compilation) that Larry first came up with the synth riff and bassline, though his name doesn't appear on the credits. Boon unleashes a series of interesting, catchy rhythm guitar parts, crisscrossing between the left and right channels. Da Costa is certainly put to good use here, unleashing an arsenal of percussion effects: shaker, bongos, *cabasa*, timbales, Brazilian cowbells and even a whistle at 3:14. During the choruses, there are also some very bizarre high-octave female backing vocals doubling Mark's lines on the left channel, though they may just be his vocals doubled and sped up. Mike's superb vocoder solo (based on an improvised scat by Mark) was performed on a Sennheiser via a Prophet-5 synth.

Bill Bottrell's bizarre remix of the track, added to streaming versions of *Standing*, uses some crowd noises from a Richard Pryor live album, Earth, Wind & Fire horn blasts and a James Brown yelp, and foregrounds Boon's Afro-funk rhythm guitar. An excellent live version recorded at Wembley Arena in December 1986 also features on the streaming edition.

'The Sun Goes Down (Livin' It Up)' (Badarou/King/Lindup/P. Gould) 4:16

This classic Level single, their first UK top ten hit, was actually a last-minute addition to the album. Larry and Verdine weren't even present at its studio conception, reluctantly going to a Prince gig at the Universal Amphitheatre in Los Angeles (28 March 1983) but leaving the band in the capable hands of the tape operator just in case inspiration struck.

And struck it did: Wally came up with the opening chord sequence and groove. Mark's ultra-sparse bassline (including a brilliant improvised lick at 0:15, repeated throughout) proved to be a bit of a problem for him when they first started playing the song live: 'I find it very hard to play the line – there are so many holes in it', he told *Guitarist* magazine in 1991. Mike came up with the melody in the verses, and Wally the 'Living it up, Living it up' hook. Mark then improvised a 'rap' – his rhythmic approach possibly influenced by Grandmaster Flash and The Furious Five's 1982 hit 'The Message' – for which Phil composed some lyrics.

The basic tracks were completed in just two takes, but Verdine and Larry had to do a little post-production work to make it all hang together (you can hear a repeated/looped section at 3:17). But it was another vital 'bacon-saving' song for the band, released as the second single from *Standing* in July 1983 and reaching number 10 in the UK. The extended version, originally included on the cassette edition of the album, features some scatting by Mark, a few extra Boon guitar licks and a long instrumental break.

The song was certainly part of the feel-good soundtrack of that summer, joining the likes of KC and The Sunshine Band's 'Give It Up', Wham!'s 'Club Tropicana', Elton John's 'I'm Still Standing' and Culture Club's 'Karma Chameleon'. But the cheery nature of the music belied Phil's lyric, an anti-nuclear tract that tapped into the frequent fears of the era (with Frankie Goes To Hollywood's 'Two Tribes' and notorious BBC film *Threads* just around the corner). Though Phil claims he wasn't influenced by David Bowie's 'Let's Dance' single (originally titled 'Last Dance'), released on 14 March 1983, that song also dealt with 'living it up' despite the fear that 'tonight is all'. The 'Let's Dance' video indeed features Bowie 'standing in a bar', singing about how he needs to love someone before they drop the atom bomb!

David G. Hillier directed the promotional video for 'The Sun Goes Down', one of the band's better efforts. It was shot in a gravel pit near Norwich, with huge piles of sand standing in for dunes, and Bunsen burners placed under the cameras to lend a more 'tropical' vibe.

One of the key singles of 1983 and one of the band's best, 'The Sun Goes Down' is played regularly in concert right up to the time of writing. An interesting remix, featuring vocals from British neo-soul singer Omar, was included on *The Very Best Of Level 42* compilation.

'Out Of Sight, Out Of Mind' (P. Gould/King/Lindup/R. Gould) 5:13

The first single released from *Standing*, and featuring another superb Alan Brooks cover design, 'Out Of Sight, Out Of Mind' reached UK number 41 in April 1983, probably a reasonable return for this likeable but slight mid-tempo groover.

It was produced by Wally at Marcus Studios in West London during February 1983, before the band made the trip to Los Angeles. The first twenty seconds of the track are pure Wally, laying down his 'stormcloud' synths and pads, and also some nice melodic lines. During the verses, Phil's snare drum is tight and imposing, Mike delivers some fine soulful Fender Rhodes, and Boon plays great contrapuntal guitar lines in the left channel. In the choruses, you can also hear the click track chugging away in the right channel. The intro to the second verse features some trademark synth work by Wally, jumping across the stereo spectrum, similar to his playing on Grace Jones' 'Pull Up The Bumper'. Mark's bass performance is typically superb throughout, expressive with a great sound.

Phil's lyric is a rarity – a love song that actually names the protagonist's paramour (Regine) and seems to be a spy pastiche of sorts ('The rain that fell in West Berlin/Was nothing like the rain that fell within').

A bizarre extended remix of 'Out Of Sight, Out Of Mind' has been included on streaming versions of *Standing*, with gated snare, less synth and no post-production effects on Mark's vocals.

'Dance On Heavy Weather' (King/P. Gould/Lindup/Bernard 'Beloyd' Taylor/Larry Dunn/Verdine White) 4:32

The rockiest track from the album kicks off with Phil's awesome voyage around the tom-toms in glorious stereo, probably recorded separately from the rest of the song. The title's allusion to Weather Report's classic 1977 album *Heavy Weather* is probably intentional. Mark plays an extraordinary flurry of harmonics under Mike's chant during the intro, and then the verses feature an almost punky bassline, nicely offset by Mark and Mike's strident vocals. A striking middle section at 2:38 features some great chord changes, and then there's a frenetic percussion breakdown with plenty of Rototoms (often manned by Mark when they played this song live). But the mixing and mastering of 'Dance On Heavy Weather' are uncharacteristically poor, the synths and vocals often audibly distorting.

Punchy and immediate, but one of the less successful tracks on *Standing*, 'Dance On Heavy Weather' was played live regularly throughout 1983.

'A Pharaoh's Dream (Of Endless Time)' (King/P. Gould/Lindup) 4:22

Although they were supposed to be coming up with 'hits' on *Standing*, the band certainly couldn't leave behind their love of classic jazz/rock. This tune, one of the album's highlights, has a double-time funk feel similar to the title track of Stanley Clarke's *Journey To Love* and features yet another brilliantly memorable bassline from Mark.

Wally gives a masterclass in synth layering during the first minute, Boon showcases some great feedback-drenched guitar, and Da Costa incorporates timbales, cowbells and splash cymbals in the right channel. Phil's drum performance is totally original, exemplified by his fill at 2:18 – he plays the same figure on snare, hi-hat and then two tom-toms. Mike's artless vocals work really well throughout the piece, and Earth, Wind & Fire regular Andrew Woodfolk makes his first appearance at 2:38, embarking on a snaky electric soprano sax solo which suits the song perfectly.

Phil's lyric is an expression of his interest in history, and his natural inquisitiveness regarding ancient cultures. In short, you wouldn't find Wham! singing about pharaohs and boy kings during this period of British pop. The band were on a creative high, and 'A Pharaoh's Dream' is a key exhibit, a thrilling mashup of funk and fusion. At the time of writing, it has only been played once in concert (at the Birmingham Odeon on 3 September 1983), but it's a fantastic opener to the original side two of *Standing*.

'Standing In The Light' (King/P. Gould/Badarou) 3:42

After the brief distant-thunder intro, Phil's bass drum is strikingly prominent and we hear yet another classic finger-style Mark bassline, double-tracked at times during the choruses. Wally supplies beguiling chord work in the verses, beautifully augmenting the basic E/C-maj7#11 chord sequence. Da Costa's distinctive 'tuned' bongos, played with drum sticks, are heard in the left channel throughout the choruses, and he also adds prominent woodblock during a very poorly-recorded middle eight, with Mike and Mark's vocals much too 'hot' in the mix. Boon plays some excellent guitar melodies in the left and right channels throughout, and there's a gorgeous Minimoog lick from Wally just before the third verse at 2:52.

'Standing In The Light' is an underrated, attractive piece that almost became the fourth single from the album, but at the time of writing has never been played live. An extended version, available on streaming editions of *Standing*, features an extra verse, more percussion and some different vocal harmonies. A fascinating demo has also appeared on YouTube, displaying all the final version's component parts but in a slightly different order.

'I Want Eyes' (King/P. Gould) 4:59

Another great Level ballad, 'I Want Eyes' was very close to Phil's heart, and his favourite song from the album. His lyric is a sad lament for wasted lives during wartime, featuring his characteristic bluntness. It's impossible not to think of the European migrant crisis of 2015 when one hears the lines:

On the beach lies a boy
Thrown away like a toy
On a field lies a man
Left behind, he was calling
No one saw him die

The opening refrain features some fine, shimmering chordal playing from Boon. Da Costa adds a varied, colourful percussion part in the first verse, starting at 0:21, with woodblocks in the left channel and Brazilian *cuica* on the right. There's some brilliant, harmonic-drenched bass playing throughout from Mark – one of his finest performances on record. He adds some intriguing 'chords' at 1:16 and then a great finger-style groove at 2:53, doubled on the left and right channels with a lot of phasing added. Wally solos excellently on synth and Da Costa switches to congas.

'I Want Eyes' was somewhat of a landmark track for the band, and quickly became a very popular live song, played regularly between 1983 and 1986.

'People' (Lindup) 4:55

Mike's second solo composition for the band started when he woke from a dream with the descending two-note bass riff playing in his head. He rushed to his trusty Tascam four-track cassette recorder, laid down the line, and then quickly added some intriguingly-voiced synth chords heard during the song's intro.

'People' was Mike's first crack at a complete lyric, and he later confessed to feeling slightly in the shadow of Boon and Phil. Indeed, his words may seem rather simplistic, but they're an honest expression of his humanistic philosophy. His verse melody is also really engaging, with a flowing rhythmic sensibility, and the microphone loves Mike's voice. Boon plays some lovely rhythm guitar in the left channel during the verses, and there's a pleasant Caribbean flavour to the whole piece, emphasised by Phil's marimba motif first heard at 0:49.

At 4:00, Mark embarks on a fantastic bass solo, very much informed by Stanley Clarke's playing style. Phil remembers walking into the studio control room when Verdine and Larry were listening to a playback of Mark's first take. The erstwhile drummer was blown away by what he heard, screaming 'Don't change a thing!'. They didn't. Phil has said that 'People', more than any other song on *Standing*, sums up the positive mood around the band during their American adventure of summer 1983. It was an extremely optimistic period.

At the time of writing, 'People' has never been played live by Level 42, but it was performed by Mike and Phil during their 2018 concert at The Concorde in Brighton (with Mike also playing the original demo to the audience), available to watch on YouTube.

'The Machine Stops' (King/P. Gould/Badarou) 4:13

'The Machine Stops' is quite simply one of the album's high points – a thrilling combination of pop/fusion innovation and science-fiction-inspired lyrics. Mark's harmonic bass chords illuminate the opening section, and he grabs the neck of the bass and 'bends' it at 0:16 to get some extra vibrato. Close listening reveals the click track setting the tempo in the right channel, starting at 0:20, and Phil's drum groove is totally original, with an ingenious hi-hat part (copied by subsequent band drummers Gary Husband and Pete Ray Biggin during live performances). The song's last minute is pure funk/jazz heaven, with a brilliant Moog solo from Wally and Mark absolutely in his element, firing off an amazing lick at 3:50.

Phil's lyrics were inspired by an E. M. Forster science-fiction novella of the same name, first published in 1909. It's an eerily prescient tale (especially during the Covid-19 crisis at the time of writing). The human population live alone in a series of underground 'cells', depending on an all-seeing, all-knowing machine for all of their technological and spiritual needs (including something weirdly akin to online shopping). Communication mainly takes place via on-screen video calls. Many people are made 'homeless', i.e. dead, when they attempt to reach the earth's surface and are exposed to the 'air'. Some of Phil's lyrics in the song echo thoughts and sentiments that could have come from the character of Kuno in the novella. Forster's story was also apparently an influence on several American films, particularly *THX 1138* and *Logan's Run*.

'The Machine Stops' is a highlight of the band's catalogue, a potent fusion of styles and a brilliant band performance to boot. The song made its live debut during the 2009 tour and has been played occasionally since.

Extra tracks

'Can't Walk You Home' (King/P. Gould/R. Gould) 4:19

The B-side of 'The Sun Goes Down (Living It Up)', and available on streaming editions of *Standing*, 'Can't Walk You Home' was recorded by Nick Launay at Eden Studios during the early sessions for *The Pursuit Of Accidents*. It was remixed by Mark and Jerry Boys at Livingstone Studios in London. Boys was Livingstone's founder, manager and in-house producer, an experienced, respected figure who had learnt his trade at Abbey Road Studios and worked with Manfred Mann, The Shadows and Rolling Stones.

The song is quite interesting musically, with one of Mark's most distinctive slapped basslines, a terrific Phil groove and Mike's excellent piano/scat solo. But lyrically it's rather immature ('You're a rich girl we all know / Daddy runs an airline'). It all hangs together very well without being essential Level.

An interesting extended version also appears on streaming editions of *Standing*, with Boon's guitar quoting Mark's 'You Can't Blame Louis' bassline, a brief, uncredited electric sax solo, and some echo effects on the bass and drums.

'Spirit Groove' (King/P. Gould) 5:17

An instrumental demo, first released on the *Living It Up* box set, this rarity sounds like it was recorded during the early sessions for *Standing*. Reminiscent of Stevie Wonder's 'Master Blaster (Jammin')', it's basically a reggae jam using a chord sequence that was later recycled for 'Past Lives' (see the chapter on *Forever Now*).

Influences (Mark King solo) (1984)

Personnel:
Mark King: Vocals, Basses, Guitar, Keyboards, Percussion and Drums
Gary Barnacle: Electric Sax, Saxophone and Flute
Steve Sidwell: Trumpet
Mike Lindup: Fender Rhodes, Yamaha DX7 and Backing Vocals
Adrian Lee: Wave PPG Synthesizer
Drummie: Drums
Bruce Dickov: Violin
Francis Mitchel: Cello
Mike Vernon, Jeremy Green, Linda Richardson: Vocals
Producers: Jerry Boys and Mark King
Engineer: Jerry Boys
Record Label: Polydor
Recorded: Red Bus (London), Marcus (London) and Chipping Norton Studios,
March-April 1984
Released: 13 July 1984
Running Time: 40:15
Highest Chart Placing: UK: 77, US: –
Current edition: 1993 Polydor

Level 42 began 1984 with a long-overdue rest, after non-stop touring between October and December 1983. Then, on 11 March, they were at London's *Hippodrome* nightclub to receive their Best British Funk Band award from the DJ Convention Of Great Britain. It was also time for Mark to deliver a solo recording. He had accepted an advance from Polydor in 1981 for the delivery of an album and two singles – so far, only the 'Freedom' twelve-inch had emerged in 1982, but now the deadline was a little more pressing: 'Polydor were actually very sweet about it, and just before the agreement was due to expire, gently reminded me that I needed to deliver an album'.

Mark explained how Jerry Boys came onboard to assist him in the making of *Influences*:

> Jerry was a good friend and had engineered some Level 42 stuff, such as 'I Can't Walk You Home', which is how we had met of course, and Polydor were keen for me to involve a third party to keep an eye on me as I was three years overdue already, so Jerry was the perfect choice. A really good engineer, plus I respected his opinions.

Incorporating ideas cooked up in rehearsal rooms over the first five years of Level's career, Mark decided to make *Influences* as much of a 'solo' album as possible, playing drums, bass, guitar and even some keyboards. But this would present a few technical challenges. Mark explained how he and Boys went about recording the basic tracks:

When push came to shove, I booked a few days at Chipping Norton Studios and dived in. I laid down the bass and drum box first. I had an Oberheim DMX drum machine that sounded awful but was a great writing tool because you could programme some pretty accurate drum parts. You have to remember that these were early days in digital technology, so ears weren't so tuned-in to accurate tempo, but I loved the idea of being able to fuck about all over the groove and lean on the drum box because it had the time nailed. I laid the drums down next – Gretsch drums, incidentally.

This was Mark's chance to finally get some of his drumming on record. As he told *Guitarist* magazine in 1991, 'I had to try and lay that ghost to rest. I couldn't bullshit my way from nine years old, telling everybody I was going to be the greatest thing ever on drums, without trying to do something about it. It made me remember how much hard work drumming is – it hurts!'. He has also commented that he was really only getting his drumming chops back towards the end of the *Influences* recording sessions. The album featured some great performances from an array of guest players (Mike Lindup, Gary Barnacle, Steve Sidwell, Drummie, Adrian Lee).

This writer didn't even know *Influences* existed until two or three years after its initial release, coming across a cassette copy in a ramshackle shop near the Swanage seafront while on a family summer holiday around 1988. It would be an understatement to say I couldn't get it onto the hi-fi quickly enough, and it didn't disappoint. The sharp 'crack' of the snare drum on opener 'The Essential' led me to believe that Phil was behind the kit, but a quick look at the album credits blew my mind: Mark was playing all the drums, guitars *and* bass? Not for a second does one rue the lack of a conventional band; this music swings, snaps, crackles and pops.

Influences is a rich gumbo of ingredients – Chick Corea's Latin/rock excursions, *Spectrum*-era Billy Cobham, Cream, mid-period Level and Stanley Clarke's prog/fusion stylings. But Mark's musical voice also comes through loud and clear. Purely from a bass perspective, it's also a milestone, foregrounding a new in-your-face tone, mixed close and loud, with hints of a 'fretless' sound here and there.

At the time of writing, Mark has not returned to such unhinged instrumental jazz/rock outside the Level 42 'day job' (apart from a thrilling series of concerts at London's Ronnie Scott's club, of which more later), but this is one of the great British fusion albums or fusion albums 'period'. *Influences* also deserves a place alongside Stevie Wonder's *Innervisions*, Lewis Taylor's self-titled debut and Prince's *Sign O' The Times* in the pantheon of great one-man-band albums.

And yet *Influences* wasn't a commercial success, gate-crashing the UK album chart for two weeks and peaking at just 77. Though sanguine about it these days, at the time Mark was irked at what he perceived as a lack of promotion, and there was a sinking feeling that he and Level 42 were not a priority for Polydor. He went to speak to the Managing Director A. J. Morris about it – a sure sign that he meant business and an impressive gesture to the company bigwigs. As Alan Sizer told biographer Michael Cowton:

> Mark was prepared not only to complain to the manager John Gould, but to anyone if things didn't go right. This was the beginning of when he realised that things could be bigger and better than they were. He had to take charge of it. He had to streamline Level 42, give the band focus and make them go in one direction only.

'The Essential' (King) 18:34
Mark explained how the album's epic opening piece came about:

> 'The Essential' began on the (Chipping Norton) studio Hammond B3 organ, which Mike Vernon informed me had been used on the Focus album *Moving Waves*. I'm no keyboard player, but I fired her up and just hit the notes. Next, I programmed the drum machine with a pattern so I could lay down some bass and guitar, and the riff and melodies just wrote themselves really. I was jamming with myself, I guess! Anyway, that's how all the sections came to be, and, in the twinkling of an eye, I was 20 minutes into the album.

Alongside Mark's crisp, Cobham-esque groove and Hammond organ, close listening reveals that Mark's slap bass in the opening section is double-tracked across the stereo spectrum. At 0:22, we get the first hint of his excellent lead guitar playing. Regarding his six-string influences, Mark says: 'I love John McLaughlin, of course, but Clapton, Hendrix, Gary Moore and Bill Connors are all in there somewhere. I love Al Holdsworth too'.

At 0:44, the horns play some harmonies which are possibly inspired by the voicings on the title track of Billy Cobham's *Spectrum*. Gary Barnacle cuts in at 1:16 with a typically potent tenor sax solo, followed by similar from trumpeter Steve Sidwell. At 3:04, there's a dash of Mark's harmonica (is there anything the man can't play?) and then a baroque vocal segment courtesy of a choir including *Level 42/Pursuit* producer Mike Vernon.

At 4:32, there's a frenetic mixed-meter section featuring an excellent Mark guitar solo, tasty 'fretless' bass groove and complex melody. Francis Mitchell's cello makes an appearance at 7:15 amongst a kaleidoscopic mixture of synths, bells, guitars and backwards vocals. At 11:45, Mark plays a bass melody that was often borrowed for his live solos during this era – a novel expansion of the 'Dune Tune' concept. A distinct Spanish influence becomes apparent at 13:00 – Mark plays some outstanding, McLaughlin-esque acoustic guitar, and Sidwell blows irresistible Mariachi trumpet. Finally, there's a brilliant 'talking' bass solo with a distorted tone, and then an outrageous, celebrated slap section at 16:04. The final five minutes of 'The Essential' was renamed 'Barcelona' and included on the B-side of a promo single sent out to advertise *Influences*.

Overall, 'The Essential' is a huge success, an outrageous display of musicianship, and a triumph of tape manipulation and studio craft.

'Clocks Go Forward' (King/R. Gould) 5:21

This excellent slice of mid-tempo reggae/funk/pop – very much in a Level style – was notable for featuring Aswad drummer/vocalist Drummie. Aswad were one of the most respected British reggae acts, and regulars on the UK and US singles charts later in the 1980s. Mark explained how the collaboration came about:

Aswad were working in the studio next door (recording their 1984 album *Rebel Souls*) and I bumped into Drummie in the corridor. I had just been running over the parts for 'Clocks Go Forward' with Mike Lindup, so I had no hesitation in inviting Drummie in to play with us. The Gretsch kit I hired had only just shown up in the studio, and there was no stool. But this didn't faze Drummie at all; he just pulled up a plastic studio chair and got stuck in. The studio floor was highly-polished parquet and it was quite funny watching him sliding around as he played! The song is called 'Clocks Go Forward' because that was the day we recorded it on (23 March 1984).

It's an uplifting, excellent piece that might easily have been saved for the next Level studio album. It was included on a promo single sent out to advertise *Influences*. Mark's bass has a 'fatter' tone than usual, sometimes even distorting in the mix, while Drummie's behind-the-beat groove and authentic taste of reggae make for an interesting alternative to Mark and Phil's insistent, crisp drum style.

'I Feel Free' (Bruce/Brown) 4:48

Released as *Influences*' lead-off single three weeks before the album release, 'I Feel Free' reached a lowly number 96 in the UK charts during June 1984, and spent just one week in the top 100. But this was hardly surprising given the fact that it received very little promotion. According to Alan Sizer, Mark was particularly unimpressed with Polydor's performance: 'It wasn't their priority. Mark actually took this harder than with any Level 42 record. It was his. He had given it his all'.

A cover of the famous 1966 Cream song, Mark claims he only recorded 'I Feel Free' as a tribute and thanks to one of his earliest heroes, bassist/singer Jack Bruce: 'He used to do ludicrous things like throwing in these Bach-type pedal things – if they stopped on an E, he would be playing a B, and you think: Bloody hell! And he's such a great singer as well. What a voice!', enthused Mark to *Guitarist* magazine in 1991.

Mark does a really decent job with his version, singing in a markedly different fashion to his usual Level style, laying down some driving bass and drums and also letting rip with a terrific, Bill Connors-like guitar break. Adrian Lee – a respected session player who had been a member of Toyah's band in the early 1980s and also worked on hits by BA Robertson, Evelyn 'Champagne' King and Adrian Gurvitz ('Classic') – also plays a memorable Wave PPG synth solo during the fade.

'Pictures On The Wall' (King/R. Gould) 4:52

Another track that easily could have been saved for *True Colours*, this is an excellent Latin-tinged funk jam, with a tricky finger-style bassline from Mark over its basic A/F-sharp/E-flat/A-flat chord progression, and a nice interlude featuring some crisscrossing horn arrangements. Sidwell features strongly again on trumpet, Barnacle plays a great wah-wah soprano sax solo, and Mike is his usual percussive self on synths. Mark's drum performance is also a mini-masterpiece, despite being embedded in various percussion instruments and a clap track, with an earthshaking fill around the toms at 3:45.

'There Is A Dog' (King) 6:26

This is an outrageous piece of musicianship that could almost have graced Return To Forever's *Light As a Feather* album. It's a bright and breezy slice of Latin-tinged jazz/rock strongly featuring Mark's acoustic guitar, Mike's Fender Rhodes and Gary Barnacle's flute.

Mark's percussion is right to the fore, with cowbells, woodblocks and wooden claves very audible in the right channel. At 1:37, Lee plays another strong synth solo, before Mark's infectious wordless vocals give way to an attractive flute/guitar melody at 3:16. Mike gets his first Rhodes solo of the album at 3:42, before Steve Sidwell plays the Mariachi-like trumpet figure at 5:00, accompanied by some lovely descending chords.

'There Is A Dog' makes for a powerfully effective finale to the album, a brilliant advert for Mark's bass, drums, percussion and acoustic guitar. It's also impressively arranged, with all the guest players getting their turn in the spotlight.

True Colours (1984)

Personnel:
Mark King: Bass, Vocals and Percussion
Mike Lindup: Keyboards and Vocals
Philip Gould: Drums and Percussion
Boon Gould: Guitars
Wally Badarou: Keyboards
Gary Barnacle: Tenor, Alto and Electric Saxes
Paulinho Da Costa: Percussion (uncredited)
Producer: Ken Scott for KoMos Productions
Engineers: Ken Scott, James Tippett-Iles and Jim Russell
Record Label: Polydor
Recorded: Genetic Sound (Berkshire), Parkgate Studios (Battle), Total Access (Los Angeles), April-July 1984
Record Label: Polydor
Released: September 1984
Running Time: 44:50
Highest Chart Placing: UK: 14, US: –
Current edition: 2000 Polydor/Universal with bonus tracks

In retrospect, it might seem strange that the band sought out Ken Scott to produce the follow-up to *Standing In The Light*. Though he was one of Phil, Mark and Wally's heroes, having cut his teeth working at Abbey Road with The Beatles before becoming a trusted producer/engineer for John McLaughlin, Stanley Clarke, David Bowie, Supertramp, Billy Cobham, Jan Hammer and Jeff Beck, Ken certainly wasn't – by his own admission – a particularly cutting-edge technician by 1984 standards. But Mark was after a 'rockier', more immediate sound for *True Colours*, and the band also wanted to learn some tricks from one of the masters.

Level were also adamant about recording in the UK this time around. Ken initially flew in from his Los Angeles base for a three-day meeting in February 1984. It went swimmingly on a personal level, but he was concerned about their lack of material. It was the same old story. Phil and Mike had been working on a few ideas while Mark was recording his solo album, but there were still big holes and song structures yet to be decided upon.

As it turned out, *True Colours* was recorded in just over four weeks. The first half was completed at Genetic Sound Studios near Reading in Berkshire – owned by legendary Stranglers/Human League producer Martin Rushent – the second half at Parkgate in Battle, East Sussex. (Puzzlingly, Rushent tells author Simon Reynolds in the excellent *Totally Wired* that he worked on *True Colours*, but there's no sign of his name in the credits.)

The Genetic sessions of April 1984 were lots of fun. The weather was great and there were games of table tennis with pop maverick Billy Mackenzie, recording The Associates' *Perhaps* down the corridor. The emphasis was on trying to capture as much of a 'live' sound as possible, with drums and bass always recorded together, usually with some keyboards and guitar too. Ken impressed everyone with his microphone techniques and instinctive feeling for organic, natural sounds. Boon was back onside, playing better than ever and more engaged with writing lyrics again. Mike was generally eschewing the Fender Rhodes in favour of an acoustic piano and synths, Mark showcased a new straight-into-the-board, in-your-face bass signal (another of Ken's masterstrokes, picked up during his work on Stanley Clarke's *Journey To Love*), while Phil was letting off some steam after the relatively slick *Standing*. Wally's keyboards were less distinctive than usual on *True Colours*, his playing taking somewhat of a back seat. Mark was on a fast learning curve in terms of studio/technological nous at this point, proud to be on the cutting edge, even occasionally advising Ken. It all resulted in an exuberant, energetic band sound.

After the *Genetic* sessions, with the basic tracks completed, Phil and Ken headed off to Total Access Studios in Los Angeles to record some percussion overdubs with Paulinho Da Costa, who had, of course, played on *Standing*. Sadly, Da Costa's fine contributions would go uncredited; according to Ken, Polydor UK were unwilling to stump up for the percussionist's American Federation Of Musicians royalties (the US equivalent of The Musicians' Union), which would have been incurred as he was the sole American musician on the album.

The Parkgate sessions – kicking off on 21 April 1984 – were not as enjoyable. The band were apparently less than thrilled with the studio and also unfortunately put up in the *Fawlty Towers*-esque, family-run Moor Hall Hotel. In Ken's autobiography *Abbey Road To Ziggy Stardust*, Phil recalled the strange breakfasts served up by their hosts: 'The eggs in the morning came out looking like some strange creature. The whole family was extremely odd...'. But 'Hot Water' was cooked up during the first few days at Parkgate, giving everyone a great energy boost. The band then jetted off for the whole of May to play concerts in Spain, Canada and the USA, returning in early June to complete *True Colours*. Then, between 19 August and 2 September, they toured Japan for the first time, supporting local heroes Casiopea. This was not an easy gig, as most audiences weren't prepared for their intensity and volume levels. As Polydor's Sara Silver told biographer Michael Cowton, 'When Level 42 turned out to be nothing like Shakatak, the Japanese promoters slightly turned their back on the band'.

True Colours was released in late September and peaked at number 14 in the UK, a lower position than *Standing* and somewhat of a disappointment. The striking cover design was cooked up the illustrious Assorted Images agency, who had also produced eye-popping artwork for Simple Minds (*Sparkle In The Rain*), Duran Duran (*Rio*) and Buzzcocks (*Orgasm Addict*). It was an exciting, intelligent album, with a host of styles and literary influences. But, according to Phil, Polydor were less than thrilled about the lyrical content of some songs, and he was frequently called on to defend the 'dark matter' that inspired the band's best compositions. The band were also now competing with huge international albums by Madonna, ZZ Top, Prince, Lionel Richie, U2 and Tina Turner – not to mention home-grown superstars like Sade, David Bowie, Queen and Depeche Mode, all of whom shared chart space with *True Colours* in the week of 7 October 1984.

Meanwhile, the band's live schedule showed no sign of letting up. Adding new saxophonist Krys Mach to the touring unit, on 12 October they performed on the legendary British TV show *The Tube* for the first time, and the next day played a *Rockpalast* gig in Essen, Germany, televised to 50 million people across Europe. A sold-out, 21-date UK tour started on 21 October, ending at Hammersmith Odeon on 12 and 13 November (where Wally was scheduled to make an appearance on keyboards, but failed to turn up). They then spent four weeks in Europe, the last gig of the year taking place on 10 December at La Mutualité in Paris.

1984 had been an extremely busy year, and the band's frantic schedule was starting to take its toll. Something had to give and changes were afoot.

'The Chant Has Begun' (King/P. Gould) 5:19

'The Chant Has Begun' was released as the second single from *True Colours* in October 1984, reaching number 41 in the UK. It was inspired by a mural on the side of the A&M building in Los Angeles – the band's record company headquarters in the USA – depicting the St Elmo Village, a charity home for deprived kids (still active at the time of writing). Welsh rockers The Alarm were apparently inspired by the same mural, releasing the very similarly-themed single 'The Chant Has Just Begun' in December 1984.

Phil took the basic theme of childhood idealism and made it another song about lost innocence and distrust of the 'adult world', laying the blame for many of society's ills on an older, war-mongering generation. It was also shot through with an anti-nuclear message and some ideas of a conservationist/ecological bent.

Musically, the song showcased a far more direct, rock-influenced sound than *Standing*, with a tight, crisp drum sound, hot bass signal, heavier guitars, rasping vocals, and synths taking precedence over the Fender Rhodes. But they still had a penchant for Rototoms – featured in left and right channels throughout the song – and Gary Barnacle was back for a typically ebullient electric sax solo.

'The Chant Has Begun' was, sadly, also blessed with an appalling video, directed by David G. Hillier, looking like some kind of post-punk prank on a PBS TV show circa 1978. While the band mimed the song, a gang of masked 'civilians' embarked on a nightmarish modern-dance routine (and yes, when the lyric mentions 'acid rain', out come the umbrellas).

A decent extended mix, cooked up by Mark and engineer Gregg Jackman (Squeeze/Chris Squire/The Moody Blues), has been added to streaming versions of *True Colours*.

'Kansas City Milkman' (King/P. Gould/Lindup/Badarou) 5:34

This was nothing less than a classic Level 42 track, with a fine lyric drawing on Phil and Boon's father's profession. The title is a riff on the idea that good journalism should always be easily comprehended by the common man, the proverbial 'Kansas City milkman'. This theme was also explored in the 1950 novel of the same name by Reynolds Packard, an American United Press foreign correspondent. But the theme is given a clever, ironic twist by Phil here, positing that perhaps ignorance is bliss: if you found out what was really going on, 'would you really like to know?'. Maybe people are better off with a lack of information. It's a very interesting lyric in the age of 'fake news' prevalent at the time of writing, and also taps into a very *au current* idea that there's too much information 'in the hands of the few'. The words also perhaps reflect Phil's experiences on the Isle of Wight, feeling cut off from the world within a somewhat parochial island environment, having to hear everything second-hand ('I read the papers/Every word/My only access to the outside world'). But he also can't help but add an intriguing Orwellian element to the inbuilt paranoia of the lyric ('The world is a stage/And we know just who you are').

Musically, the song is every bit as rich as its lyric. Mike came up with the great opening piano riff and some of the top-line melodies, also adding some tasty Rhodes. Phil plays his sixteenth-note hi-hat groove double-handed, a rarity for him, and his bass drum sounds ringy and very 'live'. Mark's bass work is superb, again with his E string tuned down to a D, many of his lines aped by Boon's guitar. Mark and Ken also attempt a primitive form of 'sampling' in the middle section, first heard at 2:39, with the use of the AMS digital delay unit which had become one of Mark's favourite new toys.

A fan favourite and a superb mixture of funk, pop and prog, the epic 'Kansas City Milkman' is played live regularly by the band to this day.

'Seven Days' (King/Lindup/R. Gould) 4:23

Though a minor track and probably nobody's favourite Level 42 song, 'Seven Days' represents a pretty unique work in the catalogue. Fans of 1980s pop will know that there was somewhat of a bossa nova revival in 1984, with The Style Council, Prefab Sprout, Sade, Everything But The Girl, Matt Bianco and Working Week all referencing the style. No one would have expected Level to follow suit, although Mike was a confirmed fan of Antonio Carlos Jobim's work.

But their flirtation with the genre works very well, buoyed by Mark's lovely opening bass melody and Boon's tasteful rhythm guitar accompaniment in left and right channels. Mark's verse melody is freewheeling and attractive. The middle section demonstrates Ken's mastery of textures and tape manipulation, and close listening reveals not one but two overdubbed acoustic pianos. Lyrically, it's one of Boon's more positive visions of romantic love, describing a kind of 'state of nature' affair taking place outside society, with shades of Bernardo Bertolucci's 1971 movie *Last Tango In Paris*.

Light-hearted and gentle, 'Seven Days' is a pleasing, if hardly essential, detour for the band. An early version, featuring Mark humming the melody, is available on streaming editions of *True Colours*.

'Hot Water' (King/P. Gould) 5:36

In a March 2020 interview with broadcaster Suzy Perry, Mark revealed that he had recently unearthed a rehearsal tape dated 22 May 1980, featuring the 'Hot Water' bass riff, recorded at his Walthamstow house-share. It had a working title of 'What About A Hot Water Bottle Waddle' and was a Minimoog/drum-machine workout sounding like Stevie Wonder jamming with Kraftwerk, but with all the component parts of the final version in place. This demo was only dusted off when an extra track was desperately needed for *True Colours*, and as such, 'Hot Water' was yet another 'bacon-saving' song for the band – a last-minute hit which bought them more time from Polydor.

The album version was recorded in April 1984 at Parkgate Studios, edited down from a fifteen-minute jam without a click track or sequencer. It was a series of great funk hooks layered over an infectious bassline, a close relative of 'Sandstorm'. Phil came up with the chorus and peppered the rest of the song with memorable lines (and it's not every day you hear a funk tune which includes the word 'impeccable'!).

For the single version, Mark decided that something a little more contemporary was in order. Inspired by watching Dick Fontaine's BBC documentary *Beat This: A Hip-Hop History* (broadcast on 12 July 1984), he and Ken Scott cooked up a novel new version with judicious use of the AMS delay machine. But it was a steep learning curve for Ken, as he revealed to *Sound On Sound* magazine in 1986:

> I feel I've been stuck away in Los Angeles a little too long for my own good. We were recording something and it went wrong, so I said 'OK, let's try it again'. Mark said, 'No, we can AMS it in'. I looked at him and said 'We can what?!'. I had no idea what he was talking about. He had to teach me how to do it. Very few studios in L.A. own an AMS, and so nobody was using them on a day-to-day basis. For that reason alone it would have been impossible for the Frankie Goes To Hollywood records to have been done in L.A.

For Phil, it was another missed opportunity, feeling that at the last minute they had finally got the sound they had been looking for throughout the album sessions: 'By the time we did that track, we worked out where we needed to be as a band, but it was too late to be able to go back and re-cut the other songs. The band sounded a bit heavy to me and was going in a direction that I didn't like, but "Hot Water" was very Level 42, and we got some of the best reviews we ever had'.

The hastily-put-together remix was duly released as *True Colours*' lead-off single on 24 August 1984, but only reached number 18 in the UK – a surprise and disappointment to all concerned. (In the USA it was the follow-up single to 'Something About You', reaching number 87 on the *Billboard* chart in August 1986.) But 'Hot Water' fared much better in Europe, going top ten in Belgium and Holland. A fairly decent video was directed by David G. Hillier, essentially a band performance filmed at the Riverside Studios in Hammersmith, West London.

'Hot Water' immediately became a live favourite, but performing it posed some problems: Mike had to start and stop the bass sequence in 'real time', which was never easy. He sometimes didn't get it quite right, and it caused him some issues around 1985. But the song has legendary status amongst Level 42 fans, and its power is undiminished today – an irresistible single with a great groove. The streaming version of *True Colours* also includes a less-than-essential ten-minute 'master mix' of the song with slowed-down vocals and other quirky extras.

'A Floating Life' (King/P. Gould) 5:05

This track kicked off side two of the original album, and it was a rare and successful excursion into rock (albeit a very slick, funky version) for the band. The main riff slams out of the speakers, but the song has some subtlety too.

At 1:11, the click track is audible in the left speaker, while Wally unleashes some lovely intertwining synth motifs, sometimes echoed by Boon. Mike's ethereal falsetto enters at 2:07. A marvellously eerie middle section features Mark's 'wobbly' bass (playing three-note chords reminiscent of Stanley Clarke's technique on tunes such as 'All Hell Broke Loose') and various interesting sonic tricks, before Phil stuns with his overdubbed sojourn around the toms at 3:37. Mark's driving bassline during the guitar solo seems like an ode to Jack Bruce, with an almost identical rhythmic approach to Cream's 'Sunshine Of Your Love'. Boon then cuts loose with his heaviest solo on a Level 42 record, sounding a little like Andy Summers circa The Police's 'Driven To Tears'. Phil's lyrics are an excellent portrait of a jaded celebrity, mentally and physically hamstrung by the trappings of fame.

An early version of 'A Floating Life' has appeared on some reissues of *True Colours*, with Mark laying down a guide vocal over a basic backing track featuring minimal synth accompaniment.

'True Believers' (King/P. Gould) 5:04

Mark's bass harmonics usher in yet another classic Level groove. The song had a working title of 'Dave Allen At Large', named after the Irish comedian's BBC TV programme shown throughout the 1970s. An instrumental mix bearing that name appears on the 2012 box set *Living It Up*.

'True Believers' features Mark's dexterous finger-style playing, with a dynamic, vibrant tone, while Phil lays down an intricate groove with yet another innovative hi-hat pattern in the right channel. The song is a fine vehicle for Boon's melodic gifts, with one memorable guitar motif in the intro and

61

another during the chorus. Mark makes his bass talk during the solo section, including a superb, 'bendy' lick at 3:12. Wally takes the tune out with an impressive synth feature.

Phil's lyrics are a distant relative of Steely Dan's 'Bodhisattva', a gently self-mocking look at the elusive search for 'spiritual truth' ('Answers on a postcard please' was the oft-repeated request of British children's TV presenters during the 1970s and 1980s). But this possibly masked a serious point about the vacuum of faith in modern western society, not dissimilar to the issues that preoccupied David Sylvian during his songs of the era.

'True Believers' is a truly virtuosic performance from everyone, showcasing the band at its powerful best. It's hard to think of any other major-label 'pop' unit who could have pulled it off. It has only been played live three times at the time of writing, most recently during the December 2011 recording of the *Live From Metropolis Studios* DVD.

'My Hero' (King/P. Gould/R. Gould) 4:17

Boon salutes Jimi Hendrix, the fallen genius of New York City's Bleecker Street, and his intelligent, sometimes affecting lyrics contribute much to this superb track. (A recurring synth/guitar melody, first heard at 1:50, even quotes the main riff from Hendrix's 'Who Knows'.) The opening section of 'My Hero' showcases a catchy, insistent bass vamp (composed by Phil) and a rare instance of Mark singing falsetto, while Mike and Mark's vocals blend superbly during the chorus. Boon contributes another excellent guitar solo (doubled by Wally on synth), exploratory and less frenetic than his usual style, ending with a lovely flurry of notes. The crashing synth chord at 3:14 – after a long period of escalating, crisscrossing motifs – is a great piece of arrangement, and the track fades out with a top-class jam session.

'My Hero' is another excellent track on a really strong album, and a deep cut ripe for reassessment. Puzzlingly, some editions of the *True Colours* CD omit the song's lyrics and songwriting credits. At the time of writing, it has yet to be performed live. 'My Hero' was originally an extra track on the CD and cassette, not appearing on the vinyl version.

'Kouyaté' (King/P. Gould/Badarou) 4:46

It's somewhat surprising not to see Mike get a songwriting credit on this, as it seems tailor-made for his talents. It was adapted from a samba-tinged group jam – recorded onto cassette during demo sessions for *Standing In The Light* in 1983 – the first half of which spawned the *World Machine* track 'Dream Crazy'.

'Kouyaté''s opening section features a barrage of percussion effects across the stereo spectrum, Rototoms on the left and in the middle, timbales on the right. Mike delivers an excellent, characterful vocal, backed up by Wally's layered synth pads during the verses. Gary Barnacle then bursts forth with a resplendent soprano sax solo, beautifully recorded and with a superb tone.

Phil's lyric is another fascinating autobiographical stew: when he was around ten years old, he had an uncle who spent a lot of time in Africa and would bring home records for him to listen to. Phil was very influenced by both the potent grooves and Mandinka dialect he heard on those albums. Kouyaté is actually a family name, roughly translating as 'there is a secret between you and me'. The resulting narrative is a tale of forbidden love with a cross-cultural twist, possibly influenced by Yukio Mishima's novel *Forbidden Colors* and Nagisa Ōshima's 1983 movie *Merry Christmas Mr Lawrence*.

When 'Kouyaté' was played live during 1984 and 1985, Mark swapped the bass for a set of Rototoms, leading to some nimble playing from Mike, who simultaneously played bass synth with his left hand, chords with his right hand and also sang lead vocals. Herbie Hancock, eat your heart out...

'Hours By The Window' (King/P. Gould) 5:04

True Colours closes with yet another excellent ballad, though Boon is notable by his absence. The opening section sees Mark triple-track his bass and use a Yamaha E1010 delay pedal for colour and depth. Wally adds some exquisite lead synth with a flute-like tone, while Phil supplies military-style snare drum, possibly influenced by his lyric. The song's title was inspired by a phrase used by Hungarian writer Arthur Koestler in his autobiography *The Invisible Writing*. Koestler was imprisoned and placed in solitary confinement when falsely accused of being a spy during the Spanish Civil War, and the experience led him to a seismic spiritual breakthrough which he christened 'the hours by the window':

Then I was floating on my back in a river of peace, under bridges of silence. It came from nowhere and flowed nowhere. Then there was no river and no 'I'. The 'I' had ceased to exist.

Phil expands on Koestler's themes of solitude and spiritual breakthrough to incorporate a romantic element, and the line 'What I'd give to see your face again' at 4:03 is a powerful moment.

An interesting early version has been added to streaming versions of *True Colours*, featuring mostly wordless guide vocals, an alternative drum performance (with Phil on brushes) and Mark's bass being sent through an echo chamber. Whilst never played live by the band, Mike occasionally plays an acoustic version of the excellent 'Hours By The Window' during his solo gigs.

Extra tracks
'Free Yourself' (Demo) (King/Lindup) 3:44

Discarded for *True Colours* at the demo stage but available to hear on streaming platforms, this is a light but catchy piece, featuring a sprightly bass performance from Mark and some effervescent scratch vocals from Mike.

'Brazil 99' (King/Lindup/P. Gould/R. Gould)

First appearing on the 2012 box set *Living It Up*, this is a gentle outtake from the *True Colours* sessions featuring Mike's wordless vocals and some typically gregarious Mark bass. The intro and verse melody are catchy and memorable, and Phil's playing is excellent. But the song lacks a decent chorus and it's easy to hear why it wasn't developed. It's well worth checking out, though.

Above: Boon, Mike, Mark and Phil in thoughtful mood during a promotional trip to New York City, 1986. *(Lynn Goldsmith/Getty Images)*

Below: Mark, Mike, Sean Freeman, Nathan King and Pete Ray Biggin on the eve of the band's 30th anniversary tour in 2010. *(level42.com)*

Left: *The Early Tapes* showcased the band's energetic, nascent jazz/funk/rock sound. (*Universal*)

Right: Joy Barling Loyla's striking cover for the classic 1981 debut album - the 'princess' - was modelled by her sister Kim. (*Universal*)

Right: The ambitious, eclectic *The Pursuit Of Accidents* (1982) featured 'The Chinese Way', the band's first UK top 30 single. (*Universal*)

Left: 1983's *Standing In The Light* was recorded in Los Angeles and produced by Earth, Wind & Fire members Verdine White and Larry Dunn. (*Universal*)

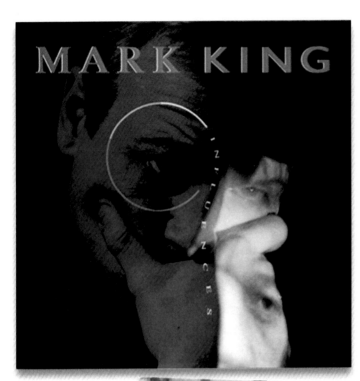

Left: Mark's remarkable debut solo album *Influences* (1984) featured his vocal, bass, guitar, drumming, percussion, keyboard and even harmonica skills. (*Universal*)

Right: The Assorted Images design agency cooked up a memorable cover for 1984's Ken Scott-produced *True Colours*. (*Universal*)

Right: The double album *A Physical Presence* (1985) was an effective distillation of the band's electrifying live sound. (*Universal*)

Left: 1985's *World Machine* showcased a leaner, more streamlined sound, leading to mainstream success via the singles 'Something About You' and 'Leaving Me Now'. (*Universal*)

Left: Phil and Mike make their *Top Of The Pops* debut miming to 'Love Games' in April 1981. (*BBC*)

Right: Mark with his favourite Jaydee Supernatural bass, performing 'The Chinese Way' on *Top Of The Pops* in January 1983. (*BBC*)

Left: Mark, Mike, Phil and Boon in the *Top Of The Pops* studio, January 1983. (*BBC*)

Right: Mike, Phil, Mark and Boon appear in David G. Hillier's memorable 'The Sun Goes Down (Living It Up)' video.

Left: Mark and Boon during the 'Sun Goes Down' video shoot – Bunsen burners not pictured.

Right: Mike, Phil and Mark filming the 'Sun Goes Down' video in a gravel pit near Norwich, UK.

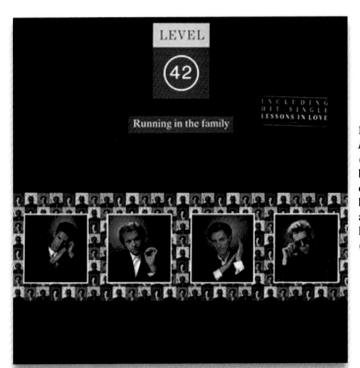

Left: *Running In The Family* (1987) was the band's worldwide commercial breakthrough, but also the original line-up's swansong. (*Universal*)

Right: *Staring At The Sun* (1988) featured talented new band members Alan Murphy (guitar) and Gary Husband (drums), but failed to find an audience in America. (*Universal*)

Right: Actress Cherie Lunghi starring with 'temperamental artist' Phil in Stuart Orme's effective 'Something About You' video.

Left: Boon pays homage to a scene from Prince's *Purple Rain* movie in the 'Something About You' video.

Right: The 'Something About You' video saw the introduction of Mark's 'clown' character, inspired by John Osborne's *The Entertainer*.

Left: Boon smiles for Stuart Orme's camera during the 'Lessons In Love' video shoot in April 1986.

Right: Mark ponders Boon's imminent departure from the band during the 'It's Over' video shoot in the Yosemite National Park, August 1987.

Left: Phil demonstrates his unique two-handed/one-footed hi-hat groove during the 'It's Over' video.

Right: Alan Murphy during the band's Prince's Trust set at London's Wembley Arena on 16 July 1989.

Left: Gary Husband takes a bow during the *Guaranteed* Tour at London's Town & Country Club on 20 March 1992.

Right: Jakko Jakszyk at the Town & Country Club, 20 March 1992. He contributed impressive guitar and vocals to the *Guaranteed* and *Forever Now* tours.

Left: Mike's debut solo album *Changes* (1990) featured an A-list rhythm section of Pino Palladino on bass and Manu Katché on drums. (*Universal*)

Right: *Guaranteed* (1991) was a return to form and featured inspired contributions from British guitar legend Allan Holdsworth. (*RCA*)

Right: Mark reunited with Phil for 1994's *Forever Now*, the band's last studio album for 12 years. (*RCA*)

Left: Alan Brooks designed the impressive *Retroglide* cover in 2006, his first Level artwork since 1983's 'The Chinese Way' single. (*Level 42 Records*)

Right: The *Sirens* EP (2013) was the band's most dancefloor-friendly collection since their 1980s heyday. (*Level 42 Records*)

Above: Mark was very modest about his remarkable ability to play complex basslines and sing simultaneously, once saying: 'It's just a case of having to do it.'

Below: Mike and Gary onstage at the Muziekcentrum Vredenburg, Netherlands, 18 February 2009.

Above: Mark's brother Nathan slotted in effortlessly on guitars and vocals during the mid-2000s.

Below: The band in full flight at the Muziekcentrum Vredenburg, Netherlands, 18 February 2009.

Above: Mark chats with Jazz FM's Nigel Williams and demonstrates the 'Love Games' bassline, July 2018. (*Jazz FM*)

Below: Mike playing his Prophet '08 during a soundcheck on the *Running In The Family* 25th anniversary tour, October 2012. (*Mike Lindup*)

A Physical Presence (1985)

Personnel:
Mark King: Bass and Lead Vocals
Mike Lindup: Keyboards and Vocals
Phil Gould: Drums
Boon Gould: Guitar
Krys Mach: Saxophones
Producers: Gregg Jackman and Level 42
Engineers: Mick McKenna, Charlie MacPherson and John Irving
Record Label: Polydor
Recorded: Goldiggers (Chippenham), The Coronet (Woolwich), The Hexagon (Reading), March and April 1985
Released: 19 June 1985
Running Time: 90:22
Highest Chart Placing: UK: 28, US: –
Current edition: 2000 Polydor/Universal

A critics' poll of the greatest live albums of all time would probably be unlikely to feature much jazz/funk, fusion, R&B or soul. James Brown's *Live At The Apollo,* Donny Hathaway's *Live* or Bill Withers' *Live At Carnegie Hall* might get a mention, but this writer would make a case for *A Physical Presence* too. Arguably, it's the nearest a British band has ever come to the kind of effortless fusion of Black Music styles achieved by supergroups such as Weather Report and Earth, Wind & Fire. It also demonstrates how far Level 42 had come as a live force – it's instructive to compare the album with some of the TV appearances of late 1984, such as *Rockpalast* and *The Tube*.

It was always on the cards that Polydor would request an official concert recording, considering the band's reputation as a crackerjack live act. And, as it turned out, the spring of 1985 was good timing; they were about to embark on their most concerted assault on the charts to date, and within six months would finally be near the top of division one in terms of British pop acts. It's hard to believe that just over two years after the release of *A Physical Presence*, the classic Level 42 line-up would splinter amidst touring pressures, musical differences and personal issues.

The band warmed up for the live recordings with six gigs in France. For security, three dates (30/31 March and 5 April 1985) were then arranged to capture enough material for the album. These were at the kinds of small-to-medium-sized suburban venues that had been the band's bread and butter since their earliest days, guaranteeing a great turnout and maximum atmosphere: Goldiggers in Chippenham (owned by Virgin boss Richard Branson and occasionally used for BBC *Sight & Sound* concerts), The Coronet in Woolwich, South-East London, and The Hexagon in Reading. The famous Rolling Stones Mobile truck was used to record the gigs, and then the material was mixed, edited and a few overdubs added at The Workhouse on the Old

Kent Road in East London, originally built and owned by 60s pop legend Manfred Mann and later occupied by Pete Waterman.

Gregg Jackman came onboard to mix *A Physical Presence* and help the band collate the material, and he does a superb job: the sound quality and mixing are top-drawer, punchy with fine stereo separation (Mike on the left, Boon on the right, just as if hearing them from the audience). But, as we'll see below, some songs are not entirely 'faithful' live performances, switching between dates and locations and featuring sundry overdubs.

Though *A Physical Presence* was recorded right on the cusp of the band's mainstream pop breakthrough, you'd never know it; it's hard to imagine any other British band before or since attempting the audacious fusion instrumentals 'Foundation And Empire', 'Mr Pink' or '88'. 'Follow Me' and 'The Chant Has Begun' hint at a new rockier direction quickly jettisoned when they got back into the studio for *World Machine*. Mark's vocals are punchy, distinct and soulful throughout, and it's hard to think there's ever been a better live British funk/R&B rhythm section than Mark and Phil. Bass players beware – this album features a succession of some of the most memorable and inventive lines in fusion history. Phil's drumming is a striking combination of groove and chops, whilst somehow also retaining a 'British' feel, somewhere between Bill Bruford and Billy Cobham. Mike gets through so much work that he sometimes sounds like he's got four hands (with a real Joe Sample/Lonnie Liston Smith influence on the Fender Rhodes), and 90% of his playing is without the aid of a sequencer. Boon emerges from the shadows with a succession of solid rhythm parts and biting, incisive solos, while Krys Mach proves himself to be a potent player and great dep for Gary Barnacle.

All in all, *A Physical Presence* is a glorious snapshot of a golden summer (though Mark later confessed to the *NME* that he was disappointed Level had been overlooked for Live Aid) and arguably the pinnacle of surely the UK's greatest ever jazz/funk/pop band. It's also a very long double album at over 90 minutes but wasn't intended to be – no one was sure which tracks to leave off, though 'Kouyaté', 'Are You Hearing (What I Hear)?' and 'I Want Eyes' unanimously hit the cutting-room floor, as did a lot of Mark solo bass material.

A Physical Presence reached number 28 in the UK album charts on its June 1985 release, somewhat of a disappointment, though it stayed in the top 100 for five weeks. Its striking cover was designed by Rob O'Connor and the London-based Stylorouge agency.

'Almost There' (King/P. Gould/R. Gould) 6:44

Recorded at the Chippenham Goldiggers on 5 April 1985, with a few studio overdubs, this latest arrangement (it had been slightly updated for each tour since 1981) makes for an electrifying opening to the album.

Starting off with the 'Hot Water' bassline sequence, but played two octaves up and with some added delay sending it across the stereo spectrum, Phil eases into the piece with an impressive double-stroke roll on the snare, while Boon threatens to pay tribute to T. Rex's 'Get It On'. Some of Mike's horn-like synth stabs were overdubbed at a later date for extra punch, as were Mark's double-tracked verse vocals and Boon's fine guitar feature. Mike delivers an excellent Moog solo before the great unison section, copied from the studio version of the song, and then there's a clever false ending.

All in all, 'Almost There' is a fantastic band performance, embellished by some shrewd and effective post-production, giving notice that this is going be a very special live album indeed.

'Turn It On' (Badarou/King/P. Gould/R. Gould) 5:47

Recorded at The Hexagon on 31 March 1985, this was a superb version of a classic single. Mark and Mike double up their vocals to great effect throughout and Mark plays a fantastic, octave-spanning finger-style lick at 1:20 in the style of Jaco Pastorius. Mike's short but effective Fender Rhodes solo has strong hints of Lonnie Liston Smith. Mark's short rap section at 3:04 is taken from his 'Freedom' single from 1982, released under the name of Thunderthumbs And The Toetsenman.

Phil's superb bass-drum flurries at 3:09 lead into Mike's synth/scat solo. The energy from the crowd is palpable, whistles and chants ringing out. At 4:00, Mark plays the famous bassline from Donny Hathaway's 'The Ghetto'. There's a fantastic hook-up between Mark and Phil at 5:26; the two were becoming almost telepathic by this point. A soothing D-maj7 chord closes out a superlative band performance.

'Turn It On' was included on the *Physical Presence* EP released two weeks before the album, reaching number 87 in the UK during early June 1985.

'Mr Pink' (King/Badarou) 6:16

Recorded at The Coronet on 30 March 1985, this was an excitingly rearranged version of a perennial live favourite. It starts with a zesty, ultra-tight bass-and-drums groove, Mark using what sounds like brand new strings. Boon chips in with some tasty rhythm guitar at 1:30, including some percussive, triplet-based chords – the whole piece is a great advert for what he brings to this band – and there's a funky Rhodes solo from Mike at 1:56. Some raucous Mark crowd banter was edited out at 4:00, and then we hear the first evidence of Phil's new electric tom-toms. Mark and Phil's final 'trading' of solos is a fantastic interlude and pretty unprecedented for a British 'pop' band.

A brilliant group performance, superbly recorded and arranged, 'Mr Pink' was also included on the *A Physical Presence* EP.

'Eyes Waterfalling' (King/P. Gould/Lindup/Boon) 5:22

This was already a classic album track, but it had rapidly become a live favourite too. The first verse was recorded at The Hexagon on 31 March 1985, then a subtle edit at 1:34 switches to Goldiggers (5 April) for the rest of the song.

Mark re-recorded and overdubbed some of his verse vocals, and his entire bass performance was also re-recorded in the studio at a later date.

Mark and Mike's voices meld superbly and there's a terrific bit of coordination from Mike during the solo section and final chorus: he's simultaneously playing the solo synth line, comping with the Fender Rhodes and also singing the chorus. Also listen out for Phil's marvellous 'catching' of Mark's bass off-beats on his hi-hats, starting at 3:53.

'Eyes Waterfalling' is another terrific band performance, aided by an impressive editing and mixing job. The final result is a big improvement on the studio version and one of the highlights of the Level 42 catalogue.

'Kansas City Milkman' (King/P. Gould/Lindup/Badarou) 7:15

Recorded at The Coronet on 30 March 1985, this beautifully-recorded track is one of the highlights of the band's career. There are a myriad of treats – Mark and Mike's unison vocals on the verses, Mark and Boon's tight riffing, the marvellously eerie middle section complete with Mark's 'talking' bass (and amazing string-bend at 3:17), and evocative Echoplex guitar work from Boon. Krys Mach plays an effective solo while Mike supplies funky Rhodes comping and a plaintive little spoken-word contribution: 'Information in the hands of the few'. Mark even finds time to include a little nod to Melle Mel's rap on Grandmaster Flash and The Furious Five's 1982 hit, 'The Message'. He also gears up for the outro with a great ascending octave run at 6:33, in a Jaco style.

A superb track and another big improvement on the studio version, 'Kansas City Milkman' also appeared on the *Physical Presence* EP.

'Follow Me' (King/R. Gould) 4:41

This was a brand new composition, recorded at The Coronet on 30 March 1985. Mark is amused by his own introduction, as he knows full well that playing the 'new stuff' in concert usually goes down like the proverbial lead balloon. But 'Follow Me' was an interesting new direction for Level, following on from the heavier sound of *True Colours*. Possibly influenced by The Police, the song was a rare sojourn into mid-tempo 4/4 'rock' and also mostly in an unusual key for the band: A-flat.

Phil's playing is a masterclass in behind-the-beat grooving, a facet admired by none other than Rush drummer Neil Peart as reported in a March 1987 interview with *Rhythm* magazine. Mark's opening wordless vocals, and various other vocal lines, were double-tracked/overdubbed at The Workhouse. The song is full of interesting licks (Mark and Boon's sixteenth-note fills at the beginning/end of each chorus) and melodic motifs (Mike's chiming countermelodies in the chorus), any of which a lesser band could have based a whole album around. As it was, within a few weeks, Level had quickly jettisoned this direction and rushed headlong towards the slick pop/funk of *World Machine*.

'Follow Me' was remixed and edited for the *Physical Presence* EP and became its lead track. An amusing demo has also appeared on YouTube showcasing a much slower tempo, with Mark's terrific bass-playing and scratch vocals.

'Foundation & Empire' (King) 8:37

Recorded at Goldiggers on 5 April 1985, with no edits or overdubs save for a few of Mark's wordless vocals, 'Foundation & Empire' sees the band go for broke with a Jan Hammer/Stanley Clarke/Chick Corea-style, through-composed epic, and they smash it out of the park. It also sticks very closely to the arrangement of the original studio version.

The track starts with a lyrical duet between Mike and Mark, with some big finger stretches from the latter, and then Mike does his lyrical Hammer-style Moog thing. Mark plays a great solo at 4:10 and then delivers a killer sixteenth-note finger-style groove underneath Krys Mach's excellent tenor feature. Also, listen out for Phil's stunning bass drum work throughout this double-time section – all of that teenage clog-wearing was certainly paying off. Boon's closing solo, utilising an octave pedal, may be his best on record, with a superb tone, strong ideas, wide interval leaps (with a superb lick at 7:50) and a hint of the Return To Forever guitar great Bill Connors.

'Foundation & Empire' is a superb band achievement and arguably the peak of their playing powers.

'The Chant Has Begun' (King/P. Gould) 6:25

Recorded at Goldiggers on 5 April 1985, this was a powerhouse performance and a huge improvement on the studio version. It kicks off with Mark's blunt instruction to the audience, and a humongous D chord with Boon showcasing a heavier tone than ever before. Phil's tom-tom-based groove works superbly, and Mark's verse vocals are excellent (possibly overdubbed at a later date).

Mike's synths during the quiet interludes have had some stereo echo added in post-production, and Mark sings some of his lowest notes on a Level 42 recording. Mach's tenor sax solo is gritty and perfect for the track, powered along by Phil's driving ride-cymbal groove and some fine Boon rhythm guitar.

'The Chinese Way' (King/P. Gould/Badarou) 4:48

Recorded at Goldiggers on 5 April 1985, this is a great band performance, if slightly marred by Mark's out-of-tune E string. Phil plays a very original lick between snare drum and top tom-tom at 2:55. Mark's verse vocals may have been re-recorded at a later date, but otherwise this is very faithful to the studio version, apart from the excellent jazz/rock-style coda at 4:27.

'The Sun Goes Down (Livin' It Up)' (Badarou/King/Lindup/P. Gould) 5:00

Recorded at Goldiggers on 5 April 1985, this is another excellent performance, though there are various edits from the original tapes and possibly some keyboard overdubs too. Mark finally gets the chance to properly retune his E string during Phil's drum intro! There's a funny bit of fake feedback added to cover up Mark's F-word at 3:16. His shout of 'Come on down!' is a famous catchphrase from the 1980s TV quiz show *The Price Is Right*. A loud 'Yeah!' from Mike was edited out at this point, and there was some lengthy Mark crowd banter edited out too.

'Hot Water' (King/P. Gould) 6:22
Mostly recorded at Goldiggers on 5 April 1985, with a few overdubs, this was a blistering, irresistible new arrangement of the *True Colours* favourite, based on the remixed single version. When the sequenced bassline chugs into life, it's almost the funk equivalent of Deep Purple's 'Smoke On The Water'. Phil incorporates some electric tom-toms during his famous break at 1:06, also heard towards the end of the track when he 'answers' Mike and Mark's vocal lines ('Here it comes again/Chugging like a train' etc.). Mark's bass licks at 2:23 and 4:10 were overdubbed in the studio at a later date. Mach and Boon's solo 'duel' is an exciting addition, and also listen out for Phil's terrific hi-hat work beginning at 5:17 – he was forever finding new and interesting ways to play a 4/4 funk groove. This superb live version of 'Hot Water' became a favourite of the band and fans alike, appearing on various subsequent B-sides.

'Bass Solo/Love Games' (King/P. Gould) 9:44
This epic medley was recorded at Goldiggers on 5 April 1985, with a few edits and studio overdubs. A long Mark bass intro has been edited out, during which he also played some excellent flamenco-style chord work. Instead, we fade in on an improvised Mark/Mike duet. By 1985, these interludes had become an important feature of the band's live encores (the crowd cheer presumably heralds the arrival of Phil and Boon onstage). Mark plays a brief, sped-up version of 'Dune Tune', then features two sections from 'The Essential'. Some of his vocals were overdubbed during the first verse, and we also get a rare chance to hear some Phil backing vocals in the refrain ('The things they really feel inside'). And what a tight closing lick from the whole band – they never rushed. It completes yet another excellent version of a fan favourite.

'88' (King) 12:54
Recorded at Goldiggers on 5 April 1985, with a few vocal overdubs, this is simply an outrageous display of musicianship and a superb vehicle for the band's strengths. It's impossible to imagine any other 1980s 'pop' group attempting it.

Boon plays some great Afro-funk-style rhythm guitar in the intro (and throughout the whole piece). Mark and Mike's wordless harmony vocals were overdubbed in the studio at a later date. After Boon's strong guitar solo, Mark takes over with a famous set of bass licks at 2:47, aped by Boon and then amplified by Mike on Prophet-5. At 9:41, Mark quotes from The Mahavishnu

Orchestra's 'Trilogy', first heard on their 1973 live album *Between Nothingness And Eternity*. Boon, Phil, Mark and Mike then contribute excellent solos.

This version of '88' was a really important track for the band, as it arguably represents their last proper jazz/rock blowout. It was also the original line-up's last ever performance of the piece. It's barely believable that Level's next stop was *World Machine*'s title track: a huge change of musical direction and emphasis.

World Machine (1985)

Personnel:
Mark King: Bass and Vocals
Phil Gould: Drums
Mike Lindup: Keyboards and Vocals
Boon: Guitars
Wally Badarou: Synclavier and Additional Vocals
Gary Barnacle: Sax
Producers: Wally Badarou and Level 42
Engineer: Julian Mendelsohn
Record Label: Polydor
Recorded: Maison Rouge 2 (London), March-June 1985
Released: October 1985 UK, May 1986 US
Running Time: 46:55
Highest Chart Placing: UK: 13, US: 18
Current edition: 2007 Polydor/Universal with bonus tracks

Despite a busy 1984 with more live shows than ever before and a top twenty album under their belts, the spring of 1985 brought a distinct unease in the Level 42 camp. Everyone had expected 'Hot Water' to do better, and everyone was looking for explanations. They were playing the same venues year after year, earning reasonable money (Phil bought his first car in February 1985, a black MGB GT) and consolidating their position at the top of the second division of British pop acts. But drastic measures were needed, and 'Something About You' was the catalyst.

It was clear to everyone in the band that the song was a potential hit, even based on the evidence of a very early demo. But manager John Gould was not so sure. He had heard 'Something About You' and various other demos destined for *World Machine*, and in February 1985 played them to Alan Sizer without the band's agreement, prefacing the preview with his opinion that he couldn't hear a hit amongst the tracks (unfortunately for John, Sizer had already heard and loved an early version of 'Something About You'). When this got back to the band, a meeting was hastily arranged at John's Wimbledon office. There was an extremely fractious exchange of views, during which he was sacked as manager of the band, an awkward but necessary move which caused a lot of strife for the three Gould brothers. Phil was reportedly the most affected.

Paul Crockford was offered the manager's job, of course already very much known to the band as a partner in their live agency Outlaw Promotions. They shook hands over Mark's dinner table and agreed on a 20% revenue split. Crockford would be a vital figure in Level 42's pop renaissance. He encouraged the need for putting on a show, projecting more of an image and doing less encores. Or, in his own words; 'Let's explode a few things and fly people through the air!'. The key was preparation, not always one of Level's priorities.

The demos for *World Machine* were mainly put together in Mark's attic home studio in Streatham, South London. In a sense, what Alan Sizer had asked for two years before (Mark taking more control) was finally coming to pass. Mark was laying down the gauntlet in terms of ensuring the songs were up to scratch long before entering the studio, but lyrics would still generally be worked on at the last minute.

Once again, the band were keen to maintain some control on the production side of things, but Australian producer/engineer Julian Mendelsohn was brought in by Mark as the proverbial 'safe pair of hands'. Mark had just guested on Nik Kershaw's album *The Riddle* (contributing bass to the excellent 'Easy'), and been very impressed with Mendelsohn's technical know-how. Wally was also promoted to co-producer for *World Machine*.

Work began at London's Maison Rouge Studios in March 1985. The band had a markedly different approach to making records now. For one, Mark was not so precious about his bass sound: 'You shouldn't be afraid of other instruments playing your lines – you've got to do the best for the song. If at a certain time it needs a subsonic bass synth, or a rounder sound than I can get out of the bass guitar, then I'll use it', he told *Making Music* in 1985. (But the new reliance on technology sometimes rubbed Phil up the wrong way, the biggest fan of improvised music in the band.) Mark was also not particularly precious about his tools, trying Jaydee, Status, Zon, Moon and Fender basses during this period. Everyone loved Mendelsohn's engineering, but according to Mike he was quite a hard taskmaster, with just one word coming through the talkback mic if any vocals were a little iffy: 'Tuning!'.

Lyrically, the brothers Gould were embracing their darker sides again, with more songs about alienation and separation (there's an album title right there ...). But also Boon's 'lighter', more sensual love songs – such as 'I Sleep On My Heart', 'Something About You' and 'Dream Crazy' – surfaced too. Phil was drawing inspiration from the more personal, esoteric lyrics of artists like The Police and Peter Gabriel, but felt his 'message songs' were often falling on deaf ears. But then the *World Machine* sessions were generally difficult for Phil: he often considered leaving the band, once going AWOL from the studio for a week. Drummer Gary Husband (of which much more later) was reportedly on 'stand-by' at the John Henry rehearsal studios in London just before the band's UK tour of October 1985.

But once delivered, everyone in the Level 42 camp agreed that *World Machine* worked. Its success confirmed a remarkably consistent collection; all the tracks are in 4/4 time and it maintains its mood superbly. Finally, the band had produced an album that Mark could compare to one of his favourites, Roxy Music's *Avalon*. For the first time in their history, a 'plan' had paid off. But it's incredible to think that they were barely five years into their career at this point. It had been an eventful, sometimes fractious period of time, and a lot of water had gone under the bridge.

World Machine's excellent cover – more akin to something Pink Floyd might have come up with at the time and quite bravely not showing any of the band's faces – was designed by the Red Ranch agency and featured Mike Trevillion's photograph of Hafnarfjall, a mountain in Iceland.

The album was released in late September 1985, immediately going top five in the UK and many other European territories (the US version, released the following May, also featured 'Hot Water' and 'The Chant Has Begun' and peaked at number 18 in the *Billboard* charts). The sold-out *World Machine* tour started on 24 October. On 7 November, Pia gave birth to a son, D'Arcy. The band played three nights at the Hammersmith Odeon between 10-13 November, and then the European tour continued until early December.

But Phil was in turmoil. As the 'conscience' of the band, and gatekeeper of their more outré musical statements, he had reportedly become concerned that Mark was thinking he was the reason Level 42 had never been massively successful before *World Machine*. Mark claims now that Phil didn't speak to him once throughout the whole autumn 1985 tour (though, in Phil's defence, he has pointed out that was a reaction to Mark not apologising for something he'd said in the press). So, although the band was enjoying an unprecedented level of success, all was certainly not calm behind the scenes.

'World Machine' (Badarou/P. Gould/King/Lindup) 5:17

The excellent title track drops us unceremoniously into Level's new sound world. It's a really cool, slinky change of direction, in an unusual key for the band (F#), and it still sounds pretty hip today.

The song was built around Wally's samba-style groove, programmed on a Linn 9000 drum machine, originally heard on his *Kiss Of The Spider Woman* soundtrack piece 'Kiss Me Now (Novela Das Nove)'. The great synth bassline is another Wally masterstroke, and then Mark's vocals enter, sounding strong and soulful. A minute into the song, there's still no sign of Mark's bass or Phil's drums. But in the second verse, Phil sounds totally at ease integrating his acoustic kit with the drum machine, while Mike plays some lovely little jazzy licks to counterpoint the vocal melody. At 3:56, Mark begins yet another of his celebrated sixteenth-note grooves.

Lyrically, Phil was garnering influences from sci-fi and horror fiction again, taking a 'God's eye' view of the world's whims and desires, and feeling very alienated from the rat race that the modern capitalist 'machine' had become. The middle-eight lyrics ('I can tell by your smile/You're no longer a child/That part of you was buried yesterday') could almost have come from Richard Matheson's 1954 novel *I Am Legend*.

Though never released as a single in the UK or Europe, Shep Pettibone's excellent remix – featuring an extended Mike keyboard solo during the fade – became a twelve-inch single in the USA (available on streaming versions of the album). 'World Machine' has also been a staple of the band's gigs to this day, usually adding lengthy guitar and saxophone solos during the outro. An excellent live version recorded at Hammersmith Odeon in November 1985 features on the Deluxe Edition of *World Machine*, as does a superfluous 'Phunk Investigation Club Mix'.

'Physical Presence' (King/P. Gould) 5:28

The excellent 'Physical Presence' is one of *World Machine*'s many highlights. An ingenious, perfectly logical Phil sojourn around a beautifully-tuned kit ushers in a classic Level groove. Mark overlays two basslines, and then Mike chimes in with his gorgeous Fender Rhodes motif. Mark's impressive lead vocal has a great deal of reverb added, and we hear Wally playing marimba-like stabbed chords, just off the beat, while Boon 'answers' on guitar in the right channel.

The first chorus reveals a lot of sonic detail: starting at 0:52, woodblocks pan across the stereo spectrum, and there's a (sampled?) Middle-Eastern *zurna* at 1:01. Phil demonstrates his fine snare drum technique at 2:07 before Boon unleashes some feedback-drenched lead lines and Mark begins his self-defeating vocal chant. The final section is 'Wally time' again, with some syncopated Moog comping and trademark 'pads', before Mike closes the tune out with some of his highest singing on record.

Phil's lyric is another meditation on relationship disintegration – a lover, friend or indeed a bandmate. The oversensitive protagonist sees trouble in every little detail ('A cold rejection/The movement in your eyes') but remembers a time when words could go unsaid without rancour ('Don't you remember/The love that filled this empty space was perfected in silence').

'Physical Presence' is a superb performance, with great playing, production, lyrics and arrangement, and everything in its right place – an unsung gem ripe for reappraisal. A less-than-essential 2003 live version was added to the streaming and Deluxe Edition of *World Machine*.

'Something About You' (Lindup/P. Gould/R. Gould/King/Badarou) 4:25

The song probably most associated with the band, 'Something About You' was *World Machine*'s lead-off single, released in September 1985 and reaching number 6 in the UK. It also peaked at number 7 in the USA during April 1986, their first and only top ten single there and a huge feather to their cap. (By 1991, it had reached one million US airplays.)

The song had a long gestation period. Heavily influenced by Deniece Williams' 1976 UK number 1 hit 'Free' (covered by Mark and vocalist Will Downing at the 1989 *Prince's Trust* concert), it was originally intended for *True Colours*. Everyone (apart from John Gould) agreed that the early demo was fantastic, during which Mark sang: 'Because there's something about you/Donna'! But the song certainly needed more work.

The opening, ascending chordal riff was written by Mike. Wally added the descending bassline which 'answers' it (first heard at 0:20) and some Synclavier backing vocals. Mark wrote the verse melody/chords and solidified the structure. Mike contributed the fantastic pre-chorus melody ('Drawn into the stream' etc.), and his voice was triple-tracked in this section.

All sorts of interesting earworms and arranging tricks were added, like the little ascending synth riff that appears at the beginning of each verse (first heard at 0:17), and also the bass drop-out at the start of the second pre-chorus. Boon's Les Paul hits the sweet spot for his memorable solo, a melody always played live to this day. It took a lot of work to get 'Something About You' sounding good in the studio, and it was apparently tinkered with right up until the delivery deadline. Phil, Mark and Wally collaborated on the arrangement, adding touches such as the triggered snare drum and synth bass.

Phil wrote the first draft of lyrics, but then Mark asked Boon to have a go. Mark preferred Boon's version, about which Phil was reportedly less than thrilled. But it's an effective set of words and a rare Level song celebrating love, but also acknowledging the work involved keeping a relationship afloat even when situations seem out of control.

'Something About You' spawned one of the band's most effective videos. Directed by experienced television and video helmer Stuart Orme (Genesis' 'Mama', Phil Collins' 'In The Air Tonight' and Whitney Houston's 'Saving All My Love For You'), it cost in the region of £40,000 – very expensive for the time. Co-star Cherie Lunghi had just appeared with Robert De Niro in Roland Joffé's hit movie *The Mission*. The video marked the debut of Mark's 'clown', loosely based on Laurence Olivier's Archie Rice character in John Osborne's 1960 play (and film) *The Entertainer*. The band play exaggerated versions of themselves; there's some amusing swearing from the 'temperamental artist' Phil, while Boon moodily riffs on a scene from Prince's *Purple Rain* movie.

One of the band's most enduring and popular songs, a live version of 'Something About You' – recorded at Hammersmith Odeon in November 1985 – was added to the Deluxe Edition of *World Machine*, alongside an underwhelming Shep Pettibone remix.

'Leaving Me Now' (King/P. Gould/Badarou) 5:03

Released as the second single from *World Machine*, 'Leaving Me Now' reached number 15 in the UK during December 1985, perhaps somewhat of a disappointing return for one of the band's most affecting ballads.

The song was primarily Mark's, possibly influenced by Roxy Music's 'Avalon', cited as one of his favourite tracks on the 2018 *Tracks Of My Years* BBC radio programme. The verse chord cycle is cleverly and subtly altered: the first time around, we hear G, A-min and F. But the second cycle is G, A and D-min. There's almost a country feel to the harmony and melody, emphasised by Boon's chiming guitar counterpoint (and lovely ascending lick at 1:31). Mark's excellent singing is double-tracked throughout, featuring some of his highest notes on record at 1:18. His memorable vocal (and bass) ad-libs, and Mike's celebrated, delay-drenched solo piano coda (sadly edited out of the single version) easily hold the attention for the last few minutes of the song.

Phil's lyric was another study in alienation, one of his most direct statements, and apparently finally submitted under some duress (an early version, available to hear on YouTube, features a completely different set of lyrics). When played live, 'Leaving Me Now' was occasionally preceded by a long *rubato* jam session which the band was fond of playing, such as the version performed at the Hammersmith Odeon in November 1985.

Stuart Orme's effective video saw the return of Mark's 'clown' character, though the bulk of it was a band performance featuring Mark emoting as much as possible, dialling down his usual carefree image. Almost impossible to dislike, 'Leaving Me Now' is finally just a really strong pop song and a fitting end to side one of the original album. An edit of the November 1985 Hammersmith Odeon performance was added to the Deluxe Edition of *World Machine*.

'I Sleep On My Heart' (King/P. Gould/R. Gould/Badarou) 4:07

Phil's slick kit-work ushers in a quintessential, old-school Level groove on this excellent track which had a working title of 'D7' (presumably a reference to one of the chords used). Wally's synth sounds and voicings somehow bring back an early-1980s vibe. Mark's vocals are strong and expressive from the outset, double-tracked in the pre-chorus section. Wally delivers some brilliant synth work in the chorus alongside Mike's appealing vocals; by this point, the band had realised the power of mixing Mark and Mike's voices as much as possible. Phil's terrific, triplet-led fill around the kit at 2:34 leads to a rather aimless section which, in demo form, featured Boon's guitar solo/melody.

Possibly a little too musically complex to become a live favourite, at the time of writing 'I Sleep On My Heart' has only been played twice in concert, both times on the 2003 UK tour. An interesting remix is available on some *World Machine* reissues, featuring an extra guitar melody and extended outro.

'It's Not The Same For Us' (Badarou/P. Gould/King/Lindup) 4:35

This is a very simple but effective album track, belying its basic B-flat/A-flat verse chord sequence, with Mark supplying yet another memorable bassline. There's a rare 'bluesy' vibe in the pre-chorus ('Every generation sees it their own way' etc.) – a section which always reminds this writer of American band Little Feat. Wally adds some cool 'Hawaiian guitar' samples in the second verse, pinging across the stereo spectrum, and the middle section beginning at 2:38 is a cornucopia of lovely synth textures. We even hear a hint of Hammond organ, a rarity in Level's music.

Phil's lyric is a slightly surreal portrait of a romantic pursuit, opening out to include his usual rallying cry for the younger generation to rise up, reject the old political order and turn away from staid negativity ('Our leaders live in the past/We can change it/There's something to hope for at last').

'It's Not The Same For Us' is a light, uplifting slice of pop/funk, but no less likeable for that, and has only been played live nine times at the time of writing. An interesting early version has appeared on YouTube featuring a different structure and Mark's amusingly off-the-cuff lead vocals.

'Dream Crazy' (King/R. Gould/Lindup) 3:53

'Dream Crazy' was modified from a samba-tinged group jam session recorded onto cassette in early 1984, the same one that spawned much of 'Kouyaté' from *True Colours*.

Mark's deceptively-simple opening riff in G, augmented strongly by Gary Barnacle's electric sax, sets Phil onto yet another classic sixteenth-note groove, probably played 'open-handed' a la Billy Cobham. There's a very catchy guitar/synth motif that answers each Mark line in the pre-chorus (first heard at 0:42), an arrangement trick that was rapidly becoming a Level trademark. Mike's triple-tracked vocals, spread across the stereo spectrum, work beautifully during the chorus. Barnacle then delivers a great solo accompanied by a fascinating little countermelody from Wally in the left channel.

Boon's lyric is a fairly obtuse portrait of a lustful love affair, a little more sensual/sexual than usual ('Dive into the neon love machine/Your body's moving like the sea' etc.). All in all, 'Dream Crazy' is a slight but attractive piece, and by now it's obvious that *World Machine* is becoming a really strong album with no filler. It was originally an extra track on the CD and cassette, not appearing on the vinyl version.

'Good Man In A Storm' (King/P. Gould) 4:36

Kicking off with Mark's bent harmonic and Wally's luscious Synclavier chord, looming like distant thunder, 'Good Man In A Storm' is a *World Machine* highlight and true fan favourite.

Musically, the verses are built around a fairly basic A/E-min/C-maj7/D/E chord progression, but Phil's lyric and Mark's melody have a perfect synergy. Gary Barnacle supplies a sparkling soprano sax commentary throughout, and Mark's bassline has a fine sense of propulsion.

Listen out for Phil's bass drum pattern during the verses – by this point in the band's career, he was becoming a master of the less-is-more groove. There's a lovely little jazz/rock jam towards the end, with Phil moving over to the ride cymbal and Mark walking the bass. Mike adds some plaintive vocals, and Barnacle solos effectively for the second time. The only anomaly is Boon's strange Leslie-speaker guitar tone, echoing Mark's bassline throughout and playing a catchy melody/solo at 3:08.

Phil's excellent lyric is a characteristically direct account of a sensitive man's reaction to romantic and familial uncertainties, with the chorus line perfectly summing up the protagonist's desire (in the face of societal pressures?) to remain gallant under all circumstances. Is it a New Man manifesto?

For unknown reasons, the excellent 'Good Man In A Storm' was never played live by the band until 2018.

'Coup D'état' (King/P. Gould) 3:42

The only thing approaching filler on the album, this is basically a jam in E with a few extra sections thrown in, but it's still a slick, streamlined classic of its kind. The title, of course, means 'uprising' or 'overthrow' in French, and Phil's lyric adroitly explores the personal cost of state revolution ('World peace at the point of a gun'). As always, he takes a forensic look at world affairs, with a natural sympathy for those struggling at the bottom of the totem pole (and, in this song, an interesting female perspective).

Phil's very simple drum groove is augmented by a battery of Rototoms, a la 'The Chant Has Begun', and a variety of percussion effects, probably triggered from the Synclavier. The sampled explosion and subsequent horn fanfare at 2:31 are very effective touches, and we close with Phil's delicious K Zildjian crash cymbals slowly fading from the mix.

At the time of writing, 'Coup D'état' is yet to be played live. A fairly redundant 'backwards' remix was added to the Deluxe Edition of *World Machine*.

'Lying Still' (Badarou/R. Gould/King) 5:42

A classic Level ballad, musically rich with great performances, 'Lying Still' is another highlight of *World Machine*.

The verses are built on a simple G-min/C-maj7 chord sequence, expertly modified and augmented by Wally's layered synths and Mark's harmonic-embellished bass performance (listen for a craftily-bent note at 3:38), played on a Zon Legacy Elite. The band pull out all the stops for a brilliant middle section at 2:50, moving from a shimmering synth solo to a flurry of various descending major-seventh and minor chords in waltz time. The closing two minutes of the song are a treat, with Mike's ethereal voice, Phil's subtle snare and cymbals, and Wally's kaleidoscopic layering.

Boon's lyric feels straight from the heart, another tale of relationship breakdown with a little more sensuality than usual and a large dash of real melancholy. 'Lying Still' was a fitting finale to the band's breakthrough album, and is played in concert fairly regularly to this day. A 2003 live version was added to the Deluxe/streaming edition of *World Machine*.

Running In The Family (1987)

Personnel:
Mark King: Bass and Lead Vocals
Mike Lindup: Keyboards and Vocals
Phil Gould: Drums and Percussion
Boon Gould: Guitar and Alto Saxophone
Wally Badarou: Synclavier
Krys Mach: Saxophone
Gary Barnacle: Tenor and Soprano Saxophone
Dick Cuthell: Trumpet
Producers: Level 42, Wally Badarou and Julian Mendelsohn
Engineer: Carlos Olms
Record Label: Polydor
Recorded: Maison Rouge 2 (London), Sarm West (London), March-December 1986
Released: March 1987
Running Time: 49:04
Highest Chart Placing: UK: 2, US: 23
Current edition: 2012 Polydor/Universal with bonus tracks

The World Machine 'plan' had worked superbly. The album had been a solid success with impressive sales and two hit singles, and its follow-up could push Level 42 into the major leagues. That, of course, meant writing some more chart-busting songs - a lot easier said than done. Mark opened up to David Hepworth in *Q Magazine* about some of the pressures involved coming up with hits: 'There was a time when I've had to sink a lot of drink to be able to drop off to sleep on Monday night. And then on Tuesday morning, you get a call at 10 o'clock to say that the single's stayed where it was. And that's it. The world hates us...'.

Mark also remembers that, to a certain extent, *Running In The Family* was the result of the record company's feeling that the band had to strike while the iron was hot. 'Lessons In Love', 'Children Say' and 'Freedom Someday' were the first three tracks recorded in response to Polydor's plea for new material:

We were out in the States and I remember the manager phoning me and saying Polydor needed something to run with because they'd released 'Something About You' and 'Leaving Me Now' at home and didn't see anything else on the album that would be a success as a follow-up single. So they were asking if we could get in the studio – pronto – and come up with something. So we had this really small window of time.

In the event, *Running* very much benefited from seeing the light of day a full eighteen months after its predecessor, since the band could keep ticking along via the three singles that preceded its release – 'Lessons In Love', the title track and 'To Be With You Again' – while anticipation grew for a new long-player. It was recorded in three spurts: March 1986 and June/July 1986 at Maison Rouge, and then 15-22 December 1986 at Sarm West (owned by star producer Trevor Horn and wife/business partner Jill Sinclair) in Notting Hill, West London. Julian Mendelsohn was retained from *World Machine* and promoted to co-producer alongside Wally and the band.

Wally was now a vital part of the songwriting team, co-penning three big hits from *Running*. Lyrically, Phil was very inspired by Peter Gabriel's 'Don't Give Up' and The Police circa *Synchronicity*, finding metaphors for his own personal sense of alienation and the divisions developing within the band. He told biographer Michael Cowton: 'I was writing about the breakup, that inevitability of separations and the loss of innocence and childhood friendships. When it becomes a career instead of a dream, other things get in the way'. But whatever was going on between Phil and Mark, they were firing on all cylinders, supplying some incredibly vibrant rhythm section playing on *Running*.

Reflected in the disparate recording dates for the album, there was plenty else to occupy the band in 1986: on 12 April, Phil married his girlfriend Lois in Copenhagen (their six-year-old son Alex was his best man). On 20 June, the band made its first *Prince's Trust* (a charity for young people founded by Prince Charles) concert appearance at Wembley Arena after a recommendation from Elton John. It was a memorable night for Mark, playing alongside one of his heroes Eric Clapton and sharing a stage with David Bowie, Mick Jagger and Mark Knopfler. Then there was a legendary Glastonbury Festival gig on 22 June, top of a bill that included Madness, Simply Red and Gil Scott-Heron (Phil remembers taking the stage just after watching Diego Maradona's notorious 'Hand of God' goal for Argentina against England in the World Cup).

The band then headed off to mainland Europe for a host of summer festivals supporting Queen, and then their US tour began on 1 October 1986, including a leg supporting legendary British singer/guitarist/keyboardist Steve Winwood (a review of the Maple Leaf Gardens gig in Toronto claimed that they had blown Winwood off the stage). They returned to the UK for four sold-out shows at Wembley Arena on 30 November 1986 and 1-3 December, filmed by Stuart Orme for the *Live At Wembley* video. They were now officially pop stars, at least in the UK – 'the most savagely brilliant pure pop group in the world today', as Mark Sinker wrote in the *NME*.

Running was finally released in March 1987. The album hit number 2 in the UK, went top ten throughout Europe and made number 23 on the US *Billboard* album chart, selling three million copies in just eighteen months. It eventually achieved double-platinum status and stayed in the UK charts for 54 weeks. It's undoubtedly the band's commercial zenith, but probably doesn't rate that highly amongst long-term fans. It also didn't garner great reviews, although Rob Tannenbaum unexpectedly gave it a rave in *Rolling Stone* magazine.

In March 1987, Mark guested on a version of The Beatles' 'Let It Be' for Stock Aitken & Waterman's *Ferry Aid* project, later receiving a personal thank-you letter from Waterman. Level's full UK tour began on 24 March 1987, including eight nights at Wembley Arena, and then there was another Prince's Trust gig (check out the version of 'Running In The Family' with Eric Clapton, Midge Ure and Mark Brzezicki on YouTube) at the same venue, during which Mark worked for the first time alongside guitarist and future band member Alan Murphy, who was appearing with Go West.

The band then embarked on a US and Canadian tour supporting Madonna in June, July and August 1987. They always had a 45-minute slot and 'Something About You' was always the second song! During the tour, Mark gave up drinking after an infamous day gallavanting around New York. Walking with crutches as a result of a tennis injury, he attended a Polygram party with Def Leppard, then a Madonna after-show shindig later on (very much against Paul Crockford's advice), during which he allegedly regularly prodded Sean Penn and Prince's managers Cavallo and Ruffalo with his crutches, telling the former that he was a lot shorter than he thought he would be! It was the last time Mark touched alcohol for seven years. As the new band tour manager Roger Searle put it: 'Security with Level 42 was to protect other bar users from Mark King!'.

After the Madonna tour, they were back on the East Coast of the US, headlining small clubs. It was a chastening experience and Boon was really struggling by now. He couldn't find any stability in his life, not helped by the constant travelling. There were builders in his Streatham home and his girlfriend had left him. He finally succumbed in September 1987, surprising everyone by suddenly leaving the band, just as 'It's Over' was being released as a single. Phil Saatchi's guitarist Paul Gendler stepped in for rest of the tour dates – Saatchi had supported Level on the recent European tour.

Phil was very unwell too. He was suffering from low blood sugar and had also given up smoking and drinking. He had a panic attack on the way to a gig in Toronto. Three days later, he had one onstage. He was prescribed Valium and then played two dates in Los Angeles (30 September/1 October) during a huge earthquake. His final gig with Level 42 was in Dallas, Texas, after which he headed to a private clinic in London's Harley Street, telling Mark and Mike that he'd be back again in time for the Japanese tour, set for early 1988. It wasn't to be. Prefab Sprout drummer Neil Conti stepped in for some Tina Turner support dates in the States between 1 November and 21 December, after which Phil decided to leave the band for good.

In the blink of an eye, Level 42 had lost both Phil and Boon. It was a huge upheaval but had probably been on the cards for at least two years, though Mark was reportedly very surprised at Boon's departure.

The Super Deluxe Edition of *Running* was released in March 2012 to celebrate the album's 25th anniversary, featuring acoustic versions, various single mixes, and the excellent *Live At Wembley* DVD from the December 1986 gigs.

'Lessons In Love' (Badarou/R. Gould/King) 4:06

Recorded during March 1986 at Maison Rouge Studio 2 (according to Mike, his early keyboard hero Keith Emerson was recording next door in Studio 1, laying down tracks for Emerson, Lake & Powell's self-titled 1986 album), 'Lessons In Love' is arguably the Level 42 song probably most associated with the band.

Mark came up with the verse chords, melody and chugging bassline (the verse melody came from the coda to the live version of 'Physical Presence', played regularly in 1985 and 1986). He put together a rough demo in December 1985, available to hear on YouTube and featuring a completely different chorus to the final one. Apparently everyone loved the verse, but the chorus and middle-eight were problem areas. Wally was invaluable here – he simplified things by focusing on Mark's verse chords, shuffling them around and adding a few more, suggesting a new vocal line. They ended up with what they referred to as the 'Sgt. Pepper chorus', thanks to its everything-but-the-kitchen-sink pandemonium and intriguing harmony, leaning heavily on the sixth note of the scale.

Wally added some lovely washes of sampled Synclavier vocal 'stacks' during the middle eight, first heard at 2:37. The final missing piece in the puzzle was the famous intro – another Wally masterstroke. It was taken from the four-bar tag at the end of the second chorus, leading into the middle eight ('Lost without love' etc.). He copied eight tracks from that section with the Synclavier and inserted them at the beginning of the song; the intro consists of sampled voices and bells, plus Boon's live guitar.

Mark explained his bass approach and equipment used on 'Lessons In Love' to *Making Music* magazine:

I'm using two basses – there's a thumb line that goes all the way through, where I use my Postman-Pat-red Status. For the finger-style line, I use my good old Jaydee – not the original, but number two, which has a great round bottom-end, 'organic', as Wally calls it. You can hear the wood in the thing, whereas the graphite in the Status suits the thumb line. It has a sort of cool, calm aggression.

But it wasn't easy maintaining the bassline through the whole song when played live. 'My right arm is ready to fall off at the end of that one,' he told *Bass Musician* magazine in 2010.

Phil used the same triggered snare drum as he had on 'Something About You', and his role was essentially making sure that he was perfectly 'placed' around the raft of sequenced percussion, Linn 9000 drum machine and slapped basses. Simplicity was the key, not always an easy compromise for the talented drummer. He does however deliver some subtle hi-hat work in the chorus, using a similar groove to the one he uses on 'True Believers' and 'Hot Water'. Boon's guitar solo – or melody – is perfect, played note-for-note in concert to this day.

Polydor MD Richard Ogden first heard the 'Lessons In Love' demo in February 1986 and was convinced it was a smash hit. He was right – it reached number 3 in the UK during June. But manager Paul Crockford initially held off releasing it in Europe, demanding that Polydor's marketing arm first develop a sure-fire strategy. The wait paid off: it was a number 1 in Germany, Switzerland and Denmark, number 2 in Holland and number 3 in Sweden, ending up as Europe's second-biggest-selling single of 1986. It also peaked at number 12 on the US *Billboard* charts during August 1987, a full eighteen months after it was recorded.

'Children Say' (King/Lindup/P. Gould) 4:54

Also recorded during the first *Running In The Family* sessions at Maison Rouge in March 1986, 'Children Say' is cited by both Mike and Phil as being among their favourite Level 42 songs. Mark has claimed that the song was influenced by Double's 1985 hit 'The Captain Of Her Heart', but the track's roots were in a bassline cooked up during a soundcheck for the Hammersmith Odeon shows in October 1985.

Wally demonstrates his mastery of synth pads in the verses, played with a Roland RD-300 digital piano. There's a lot of space, leaving one to focus on Mark's excellent vocals – clear with good diction. Phil lays down a minimalist groove, but there are also some ingenious overdubbed snare-drum fills (particularly one at 0:11). His affecting lyric touches again on innocence, the youth possessing almost a mystical, telepathic instinct ('We open our minds as one'), with shades of *Standing In The Light*'s title track and 'The Chant Has Begun'.

'Children Say' was released as *Running In The Family*'s fifth single – in truncated form, with an added lead guitar melody (possibly played by Mark?) – during December 1987, reaching a rather disappointing number 22 in the UK but making the top ten in the Netherlands. The video is interesting; at the time of filming, Phil and Boon had just left the band, so we see Mark and Mike trying to keep things together during a difficult time, hamming it up with the Parisian public.

The excellent 'Children Say' remains a popular live song, played regularly to this day, often with an extended instrumental intro and outro.

'Running In The Family' (P. Gould/Badarou/King) 6:14

The album's title track very much divides opinion. To some, like this writer, it's close to the nadir of the band's recording career. To others, it's pure pop fun. Mark reportedly isn't a huge fan of the song, but Mike still has some time for it.

According to Mark, the whole verse melody came to him in one go, and his rock-with-slap-bass groove is possibly inspired by Stanley Clarke's approach on tracks such as 'School Days', 'My Life' and 'Old Friends'. Krys Mach's electric sax motif is catchy and novel, while Boon plays some great, muted rhythm guitar in the left and right channels throughout the first verse (heard at 0:31) and a clever countermelody during the choruses.

Mike's vocals are uncharacteristically 'pitchy' in the chorus, and this is one song in which his and Mark's voices don't gel effectively. Phil's snare drum is augmented by the now-ubiquitous explosive trigger effect and he sounds very restricted, though there's a terrific moment at 5:07 when his sixteenth-note hi-hat 'barks' are echoed two beats later by Mark's bass. Even the band's most blatantly commercial tracks still contained moments of sublime musicianship.

Phil's lyrics are not autobiographical, but clearly the whole subject of family ties had been on his mind, not surprising given the recent sacking of his brother John and impending schism of the original band line-up. The words take a comic look at the roles we play in family life and the power games that emerge. A fascinating early version has recently appeared on YouTube featuring a completely different set of lyrics, including this bizarre line which opens the second verse: 'I've got a movie in my head/Watch it in my bed/I always play the starring role'. This scratch lyric was sung by Mark during a performance of 'Running In The Family' at the Wembley Arena in December 1986 (available to watch on YouTube). Phil may also have been inspired by Michael Ondaatje's 1982 book of the same name, a semi-fictional memoir focusing on the author's return to his native island of Sri Lanka during the late 1970s.

'Running in the Family' was released in February 1987 as the second single from the album, reaching number 6 in the UK. Stuart Orme's rather brash video is a difficult watch these days, Phil and Boon looking particularly uncomfortable while Mike and Mark do their level best to sparkle.

'It's Over' (King/R. Gould/Badarou) 6:01

The fourth single from the album, 'It's Over' reached UK number 10 in September 1987. It was in some ways a brave choice, more downbeat even than 'Leaving Me Now'. The song's feel and textures were possibly influenced by Roxy Music's 1982 single 'Avalon', though its verse melody and harmony also have almost a country and western vibe, emphasised by the pedal-steel guitar and harmonica added to the single version.

The first 40 seconds of the song are pure Wally magic, a 'greatest hits' selection of his synth sounds. Boon plays some rather odd Mu-Tron-infused rhythm guitar, but Phil comes up with yet another ingenious drum performance, playing sixteenth notes on the hi-hat both with his foot and sticks (he demonstrates the groove in the song's video). In fact, the bass and drums are just terrific throughout, expressive with a lovely 'loose' feel. Even if other aspects of their relationship were suffering, Mark and Phil obviously still had a near-telepathic musical understanding.

There's a rare use of a 'bittersweet' major-seventh chord at end of each chorus, first heard at 2:09, and Boon delivers another heartfelt, direct lyric, one that turned out to be very prescient. Mark recalled flying over Yosemite Park in Colorado to film the video, having just been told that Boon would soon leave the band. It was quite a surprise, as he had always assumed Phil would be the first of the Gould brothers to depart. But Boon's penultimate appearance with Level 42 (until a live guest appearance in 2012, of which more later) took place on 4 September 1987 when he mimed 'It's Over' on BBC1's *Wogan* programme. It was an underwhelming finale for a key founder member who had contributed so much to the group, and would continue to do so from the sidelines.

'To Be With You Again' (King/R. Gould) 5:19

Kicking off with Phil's two hi-hats, this is one of Mark's all-time favourite Level 42 songs. It was the third single from *Running In The Family*, and another UK number 10 in May 1987. In March of that year, Mark had proudly played it for presenter Andy Peebles during a BBC Radio 1 interview, saying he had 'high expectations' for the track. In 2010, he told *The Herts Advertiser* more about its roots:

> There's something heroic about it. It was originally called 'Berlin Baby'. It's just a great autobiographical lyric for Boon – I think that's how he was feeling about all the work we were doing at the time. Funnily enough, it's a bit of a precursor because a year later he wanted out. He did one set of lyrics but was asked to have another crack at them, as he was sure it could be a hit.

Mark came up with an exceptionally complex bassline for 'To Be With You Again', belying its quite basic chord changes. This posed some problems when playing it live, as he explained to *Bass Musician* magazine: 'You lay the bass parts down as best you can, then a little while later you lay down the vocals and go to town on that, then a little while later you go into rehearsals for the tour and then it's... "Mother of God, this is tricky!". But you just have to get on with it'. Mark has had a lot of practice getting on with it – the song has become somewhat of a live favourite.

Stuart Orme's video was a tongue-in-cheek portrait of Boon's military-themed lyric, with the band donning Napoleonic uniforms and generally larking about. Mark was in the mood for dressing up and having some fun, but some of the band weren't, as he told *The Herts Advertiser*:

> I liked the Napoleonic thing. I said, can we have something a bit flamboyant and colourful, and the wardrobe department came up with these things and we just jumped into them and we had a bit of a laugh. Then we went out to the Montreux Pop Festival, which was this big televised thing they used to do off the lake there, and we thought we'll just have the uniforms flown out. But Phil just refused point-blank to wear the stuff, so I put mine on, and I think Boon put his on, and there were a lot of the other artists tittering and thinking it was a really bizarre thing to do, but I never saw it as that. You're as out-there as you need to be.

Despite Mark's fondness for 'To Be With You Again' and the excellence of the band performance, these days it sounds very much like 'Level by numbers', almost a pastiche of their late-80s sound, a compendium of major chords and complex basslines that generally flatters to deceive.

'Two Solitudes (Everyone's Love In The Air)' (King/P. Gould/Lindup) 5:37

A relatively unsung classic from the album, and a welcome change of pace, 'Two Solitudes' started life as a Mike chord progression, the one heard at the outset. Mark then contributed the verse melody, and they composed the chorus together. The inclusion of Boon's acoustic guitar is a great touch, as is his nicely understated solo. Mark detunes his E string down to a D and delivers a marvellously nuanced bass performance, perfectly meshing with Phil. One could listen to these two play all day. Mike's lead vocal is excellent, understated but full of character, expertly double-tracked in the chorus, and it's refreshing to hear Mark singing a higher harmony than Mike at 1:03. Also, listen out for Wally's 'steel drum' sample offering a pleasant melodic counterpoint during the second and third choruses (first heard at 2:19).

Lyrically, the song is a close relation to 'Physical Presence', another of Phil's studies in alienation and lost trust. There's also a reference to Rudyard Kipling's poem 'If' ('Now we meet those two impostors just the same'). A demo of 'Two Solitudes' has appeared on YouTube, featuring Mark on lead vocals. The track has only very rarely been performed live by the band, most recently in 2013, though Mike occasionally plays it during his solo gigs.

'Fashion Fever' (King/R. Gould/P. Gould/Lindup) 4:35

Phil's crisp snare drum kicks off this song which, again, is very much 'Level by numbers', a rather rushed facsimile of the up-tempo *World Machine* tracks but lacking a strong through-line or hook. You can feel *Running* rather 'creaking' along at this point, but the playing is so good that it almost doesn't matter.

'Fashion Fever' was essentially Mark's baby; he provided a very basic home-recorded demo (available to hear on YouTube) which featured his vocals proclaiming the occasional 'It's that feeling!' in place of the final lyric. Phil and Mike worked on the middle-eight (Mark's demo featured a rap at that point) and there was a chance for Boon to unleash a really biting, incisive solo (the second half of which is audibly 'punched in' at 2:31). Phil's use of hi-hats and crash cymbals is fantastic, as is his snare drum technique, typified by the little single-stroke roll at 1:28. 'Fashion Fever' was arguably the adrenalin-fuelled peak of his playing with the band - sadly right at apex of his involvement - with subtlety, flair, dynamics and chops.

Boon also contributed a lyric which, to be generous, is not one of his better efforts – an attempt at satire which unfortunately lands more as a rather immature statement from the 'I Can't Walk You Home' file ('You look in Vogue to seek the scene/Try looking through the pages again' etc.).

The strangely underwhelming 'Fashion Fever' was played regularly during the 1986 and 1987 tours and was occasionally the opening song.

'The Sleepwalkers' (King/P. Gould) 6:02

In the classic mid-tempo, half-time style that had become the band's trademark,

'The Sleepwalkers' was mainly concocted in the studio: a rarity at this point and something that Mark was generally uncomfortable with. And perhaps the lack of preparedness shows – it has an unfinished, underwhelming quality, and seems a little leaden.

Mark's home demo featured a sequence of sampled harps and log drums (heard at the beginning of the second verse). Phil was apparently very taken with it and quickly wrote an ironic, gently self-mocking lyric; by 1987, Phil was very rarely seen without his Ray-Bans in public (though he claimed this was for medical reasons), comparing the wearers of sunglasses to a nation of sleepwalkers and sensation seekers. But he does come up with some surreal, funny lines ('I have a game plan/But my love is in a jar'!).

Mark detunes his E string right down to a C (this was before he was using five-string basses) and Mike contributes a strange Farfisa organ part during the choruses. Vocally, it's a really strong song; Mark's performance has good diction and some neat, jazzy phrasing ('Though I don't think like you do'), and Mike and Mark combine to provide bluesy backups in the chorus. Phil's two-hi-hat groove is original, but his playing feels a little hamstrung by everything going on around him. In terms of his musical fulfilment, this is the kind of track that might have been the straw that broke the camel's back.

'The Sleepwalkers' wasn't played in concert until 2001 and has only been revived very occasionally since then.

'Freedom Someday' (King/R. Gould/P. Gould/Lindup) 6:20

Recorded during the initial *Running* sessions at Maison Rouge in March 1986, this was the band's first half-time shuffle and the song made for an interesting, upbeat departure. There's a lot of space in the verses: Mark's excellent, jazzy vocal melody, driving bassline and backing vocals (in a higher register than normal), Mike's four-to-the-bar synth chords, a few Boon rhythm guitar parts (developing in the right channel during the second verse) and Phil's minimalist groove.

After the first refrain, Dick Cuthell plays an excellent muted trumpet solo, obviously under the influence of Miles Davis. He was an experienced session player, best known for his work with The Specials, Eurythmics and Madness. Also listen out for Phil's intricate, ghost-noted fill at 5:43, in the style of US drumming great Jeff Porcaro.

'Freedom Someday' was a refreshing change of pace for the band, light in tone with a bouncy feel and breezy melody, but was not originally included on the vinyl version of *Running*, appearing as an extra track on CD and cassette. It was never played live by the original line-up, only surfacing occasionally on the 2012/2013 tour.

Staring At The Sun (1988)

Personnel:
Mark King: Bass and Lead Vocals
Mike Lindup: Keyboards and Vocals
Gary Husband: Drums and Percussion
Wally Badarou: Keyboards
Alan Murphy: Guitar
Dominic Miller: Guitar
Krys Mach: Saxophone
Steve Sidwell: Trumpet
Producers: Wally Badarou, Level 42 and Julian Mendelsohn
Engineer: Julian Mendelsohn
Record Label: Polydor
Recorded: Chateau Miraval (France), March-April 1988
Released: September 1988
Running Time: 49:41
Highest Chart Placing: UK: 2, US: 128
Current edition: 2014 Polydor/Universal with bonus tracks

Early 1988 was a transitional period for Level 42. Phil and Boon had left at the apex of the band's commercial viability, at least in the UK and Europe, but the thought of pulling the plug had never even crossed Mark's mind. It was a time to take control and work with some new people. And, if the fly-on-the-wall documentary *Fait Accompli* (of which much more later) is anything to go by, he was in a great mood, sober, settled and full of beans, enjoying some fresh career challenges. Polydor had made a big commitment to Mark and Mike, but the clock was ticking too – the label wanted the collection that would finally 'break' Level 42 in America. After all, they had achieved two hits over there, but the CD revolution ensured that the album was going to be the future, not the single.

On 3 January 1988, Mark and Mike convened at The Warehouse, a rehearsal space in Dublin's Lotts Lane (they were taking a year out of the UK for tax purposes), to prepare for upcoming gigs in Israel and the Far East. Mark had been writing much of *Staring At The Sun* there, sending Boon the demos to add his lyrical input. And now they had two new band members in tow: guitarist Steve Topping (who wouldn't stay in the line-up beyond the brief tour of early 1988) and drummer Gary Husband.

Gary was born in Leeds in 1960. He was encouraged to study classical piano by his musician father but also had half an ear on the rock and jazz/ fusion sounds of the late 1960s, with a particular penchant for Jimi Hendrix. Inspired by Mitch Mitchell, Tony Williams and Billy Cobham, Gary moved over to the drum kit, immediately feeling right at home, and his dad helped him get a jazz gig with The Syd Lawrence Orchestra in 1976 (you can watch sixteen-year-old Gary's incredible performance of 'Drumming Man' on

YouTube). He moved to London at the age of eighteen, picking up work in funk, metal, pop and jazz bands. Gary was performing with British jazz legend Barbara Thompson at London's Ronnie Scott's club in 1980 when he met guitarist Allan Holdsworth. Holdsworth was, of course, one of the most innovative axemen of the 1970s, famous for his fiery, horn-like 'legato' technique and groundbreaking work with Tony Williams' Lifetime, Nucleus, Gong, Bill Bruford and Soft Machine. Holdsworth and Husband got together for a life-changing jam session and became both regular collaborators and great friends (Holdsworth albums *Metal Fatigue, Wardenclyffe Tower, Then, Atavachron, I.O.U., Sand* and *Hard Hat Area* are essential listening for evidence of their electrifying guitar/drums interplay).

Mark had watched Gary's performance of 'Drumming Man' on TV in 1977, and when Phil started making noises about leaving the band, Gary's name came to mind. He first nearly joined Level 42 in October 1985, and then again just before the Madonna support tour in summer 1987. But his official signing as a full-time member in December of that year certainly wasn't an easy transition into the pop arena, and Gary wasn't always given an easy ride by hardcore fans:

This was long before the internet and social media, bear in mind. Paul Crockford would dish out letters from a large black plastic bin bag in his office. I got mail that was absolutely toxic! "Please leave the band! We don't want you! You're a jazz/fusion drummer, not a funk drummer!" That's a hint that doesn't involve all the juicy personal insults and foul language! But that's natural, I guess. When you change a drummer in a band, you change everything. Simon Phillips had his fair share of heat replacing Jeff Porcaro in Toto. Then Keith Carlock joined and got hit with being no kind of replacement for Simon Phillips! Perhaps my own situation was a bit more akin to Narada Michael Walden replacing Billy Cobham in The Mahavishnu Orchestra, because it was a new band and new music. But that stuff isn't to be taken to heart. Though, I do have to say, in that period I was met with by far the ugliest and toughest criticism I've ever experienced in any musical situation! And I've been in a fair few! You can't please everyone. Plus, and I have to maintain this, I wasn't anything like as great as I aspired to be in the band, and, with hindsight, was regularly way too exuberant in what I brought to the music. Either that or often just not quite right. But I'm happy having been Gary Husband in a challenging role and not some clone attempting to try and play like Phil Gould – should that possibility even have been within my grasp!

The new four-piece's first gigs took place in Tel Aviv on 23/24 January 1988. They moved on to Japan, Singapore and Indonesia in February and March, including a memorable show in Jakarta. They finally landed back in Dublin to finish writing *Staring*, and then spent four weeks recording at Chateau Miraval in Le Val, Southern France: a studio on a wine-making estate owned by Third Stream piano pioneer Jacques Loussier, world famous for his jazzy Bach interpretations. Previous Miraval residents included Pink Floyd (*The Wall*), David Sylvian (*Secrets Of The Beehive*) and Wham! (*Make It Big*). *World Machine* co-producer Julian Mendelsohn was back on board alongside Wally, and both Dominic Miller and Alan Murphy joined as session guitarists. Alan's playing and personality immediately impressed everyone, and he quickly accepted Mark's offer to become a permanent member of the band. Saxophonists Gary Barnacle and Krys Mach were retained from *Running*, and newcomer Steve Sidwell joined on trumpet. Boon was also invited to stay at the Chateau for the duration of the recording sessions.

Mark's new songs represented the band's 'rockiest' material to date. More guitars were called for (some played by Mark), and there was less space for intricate bass/drums interplay or saxophone solos. But the recording went particularly smoothly (maybe too smoothly), and everyone – including Polydor – seemed pretty happy with the results. *Staring*'s impressive album artwork and design were cooked up again by Stylorouge – possibly a visual representation of the song 'Man' and a huge improvement on *Running*'s humdrum effort, though with hindsight one wonders whether the choice not to feature the band's faces on the cover hindered the package and diluted the Level 42 'brand' (the back cover photos were a different story altogether – see the later section on *Fait Accompli*).

Mark, Mike, Alan and Gary headed back to London for two *Prince's Trust* gigs at the Royal Albert Hall on 5/6 June 1988, acting as the house band for all of the guest artists (except for Van Morrison, who reportedly refused to work with them!). Around this time, Mark also moved from London back to the Isle Of Wight, finding a large, comfortable house at the edge of Rye, set in seven acres of land. Meanwhile, work got underway on the *Fait Accompli* documentary.

Staring was released in September 1988, immediately hitting number 2 in the UK (equalling *Running*'s performance), number 1 in the Netherlands and number 8 in Germany. The omens were looking good, but the album didn't take off in the USA, reaching just 128 on the *Billboard* chart. But the forthcoming UK and European arena tour was all but sold out, proving that Level had never been more popular as a live act.

There were other reasons for celebration: Mark's first daughter Jolie was born on 2 October 1988, just before the Dutch leg of the tour. On Tuesday 6 October, Mark received a call from Paul Crockford saying that *Staring* had gone platinum, but tempered it (according to band biographer Michael Cowton) with the memorable phrase: 'You've only sold a million albums'! Apparently the plan had been for five million. But this was probably unrealistic – there was now serious British competition in the USA from Phil Collins, OMD, Depeche Mode, Rick Astley, ABC, Pet Shop Boys, Sting and George Michael. It was also probably a tall order for Level to get some serious commercial traction without a movie tie-in, and with the likes of Debbie Gibson, Tiffany and New Kids On The Block eating up the American charts.

However, one still wonders if the *Staring* material was strong enough. It was certainly recorded very quickly by 1988 standards. The vultures were circling. As reported in the *Fait Accompli* documentary, Mark was set up in a tabloid 'sting', and the album predictably received poor reviews in *Melody Maker* and *NME*. *Q Magazine* was ambivalent, calling *Staring* 'out of kilter from the off', but praised its quieter moments.

'Heaven In My Hands' (King/R. Gould) 4:42

The bombastic 'Heaven In My Hands' was the lead-off single from *Staring*, released in August 1988 and reaching number 12 in the UK, though not charting in the USA. Mark spoke of his irritation when meeting record pluggers in Los Angeles who would listen to the track and throw their hands up in despair, saying, 'You guys are all over the place!'. But this was after everyone had been telling them that you had to have more guitars and louder drums in order to break America!

The music for 'Heaven In My Hands' was written by Mark at the Gresham Hotel in Dublin, and then sent to Boon for his lyrical input. According to Mark, Steve Sidwell's opening trumpet fanfare was inspired by some incidental music from the cult 1960s TV series, *The Prisoner*. Alan makes his presence felt with some cracking delay-drenched guitar in the left channel, in the 'percussive' style of David Gilmour and John Martyn. Gary's drum sound is huge, a very different proposition to anything else in the Level catalogue, and his playing is precise and powerful. Mark's verse bass riff is fairly simplistic and unoriginal though, almost like the Level version of Michael Jackson's 'Bad', though he does let fly with a notable slapped lick at 0:42. Mike adds a few neat motifs, like the synth trills beginning at 1:28, and then Murphy plays a great (albeit brief) solo, with a great lick across the bar line at 3:45, in the style of Jaco Pastorius or Biréli Lagrène. Boon's lyric is a study in self-doubt, a painfully honest portrait of a wasted life.

The intro to the extended remix (included on streaming versions of *Staring*) was used by the BBC for their 1989 coverage of the Wimbledon tennis championships. Polydor spared no expense in trying to make 'Heaven In My Hands' a hit (though of course the bill would eventually be charged back to the band...): Steve Barron, director of The Human League's 'Don't You Want Me', Michael Jackson's 'Billie Jean', A-ha's 'Take On Me' and Dire Straits' 'Money For Nothing', helmed the impressive video, shot in a New Orleans suburb during the sweltering July heat.

'I Don't Know Why' (M. King/R. Gould) 4:24

The second track from *Staring* was a rather peculiar reggae/pop song found at the bottom of The Police's demo drawer. The guitar riff doesn't maintain much interest, and Mike's synths sound a little passé for the first time in the band's history. The bass/synth bass combination is very restricting, and the Middle Eastern-tinged vocal melody somewhat underwhelming. Mark's reggae 'toasting' is ill-advised and Mike tries in vain to add some interest with a myriad of vocal motifs. The only light relief occurs at 1:58 when Gary injects an amusingly-outré snare fill leading into the middle eight. Boon's lyric is also not one of his strongest: one wonders if it's an attempt at pastiche, but it's hard to tell. All in all, 'I Don't Know Why' is a rushed, undercooked track that lacks a decent chorus or hook. At the time of writing, it hasn't been performed live.

'Take A Look' (King/Lindup/R. Gould/Badarou) 4:42

Heavily under the influence of Todd Rundgren, Mark's favourite new artist, 'Take A Look' is a strong, beguiling composition with very clever use of minor/ major chords and not one but two modulations (including a great, unexpected one in the middle of the second chorus at 2:10), possibly reflecting Wally and Mike's songwriting contributions. But one can't help wondering whether the track is slightly undone by its 'funkiness', ubiquitous synth bass and grating synth sounds.

Alan Murphy supplies the attractive harmony lead guitars during the chorus, sounding a little like Boon, and Mark's vocal is impressive, including a particularly powerful line at 3:34 ('You must surely know/If man made heaven then man made hell'). Boon's lyric is generally one of his more effective on the album, a sad little tale about how a happy, if somewhat naive man is corrupted by a corrosive love affair. David Hogan (Prince's 'U Got The Look' and Diana Ross's 'Eaten Alive') directed the expensive-looking video, filmed during the band's summer sojourn in New Orleans. It was attractively shot if a little lacking in the story department.

Released as *Staring*'s second single in October 1988, 'Take A Look' reached a rather disappointing number 32 in the UK charts, and was played regularly throughout the subsequent world tour. A very strange extended remix has been added to streaming and Deluxe versions of the album.

'Over There' (King/Lindup) 4:02

A very rare Level track with a 6/8 time signature, 'Over There' can only really be defended as a vehicle for Gary's powerful, probing jazz/rock drums. It's a peculiar song and a bit of a dog's dinner, centred around Mark's 'strumming' of the pat, folk-style verse chords (A/G/D/E-min) on his bass. Lyrically, it seems a close relation to 'To Be With You Again', another tale of love during wartime. A strange mix of folk, jazz/rock and pop, 'Over There' was nowhere near the kind of 'fusion' Level fans were after at this point, but it was played live throughout the *Staring* tour.

'Silence' (Lindup) 5:00

Mike's solo composition on *Staring* is sadly another disappointment, featuring a fairly predictable chord sequence and dated bass-synth sound. But he adds some lovely Caribbean-style interjections in the third verse and subsequent chorus. Sounding like it was recorded very quickly, the best thing about 'Silence' is the lyric: Mike's typically empathetic survey of love's rejections and insecurities with a strong, positive closing message. It was performed live throughout the *Staring* tour, and a live version featuring some excellent Alan Murphy guitar is included on the streaming/Deluxe edition of the album.

'Tracie' (King/Husband) 4:52

This infectious, upbeat song with almost a go-go groove was the third and final single from the album (with a cover photo by Linda McCartney), reaching UK number 25 in January 1989. Gary explained the genesis of the piece:

> It was Mark's already-existing music and melody line, and I was given the task of coming up with some lyrics for it. Lyrics weren't ever an area of strength for me, but regardless of what I consider to be the quality of them, I made a go of it overnight and they were recorded the very next morning. My results were what they were. Maybe they've got a bit of that rather naff, 'bubblegum' appeal that some songs by even very notable artists have done very well with. I really don't know. I hadn't, and still don't, have any expertise or flair to speak of in the lyric-writing realm.

It has to be said that the song didn't do a lot for Level's rather dodgy image in the UK around 1988; there were a fair few highly condescending 'Sharon and Tracie' jokes echoing around the school playground, for better or worse. But Mark was having a great time, emphasised by his horseplay in the song's freewheeling video. 'Tracie' was performed throughout the *Staring* tour. Two extended remixes can be heard on streaming versions of the album, one featuring some superb new guitar from Alan Murphy and a surreal rap by Mark.

'Staring At The Sun' (King/R. Gould/Badarou) 4:43

Staring's title track is a funereal ballad, certainly not one of the band's strongest. It stumbles along in a wash of soggy synths and sampled timpani, and features a peculiarly-chorded middle section at 1:34 with Mike's double-tracked vocals and stacked trumpets from Sidwell. Some light relief is provided at 2:35 when Krys Mach enters for a classy, if very brief, tenor sax solo. Mark's rather restrictive, elongated melody lines give Boon a tough job with the lyrics, and sadly he can't come up with much beyond some rather absurd lines such as: 'Like a burning spear of stars falling/ You dissolve the night in tears/ So tired'. The song and album title were possibly inspired by Julian Barnes' 1986 novel of the same name. 'Staring At The Sun' is both ponderous and portentous, certainly not words you'd usually associate with Level 42. At the time of writing, it hasn't been played live.

'Two Hearts Collide' (King/R. Gould) 4:12

Unfortunately, things don't improve too much with this unprepossessing mid-tempo rocker. The melody is fairly inert, the rhythm track limpid and the lyric's central metaphor hackneyed. It's one of the most mystifying tracks in the Level catalogue. Just what is it influenced by? And who is it intended for? Who knows? It's possibly an attempt to appeal to the American market, but Dominic Miller's guitars aren't loud enough and Mark's vocals never get out of second gear. It also seems to be searching for the 'heroic' chorus which never arrives. 'Two Hearts Collide' has yet to be played live at the time of writing, but Tom Lord-Alge's extended remix has been added to streaming/Deluxe versions of the album, foregrounding Miller's rhythm guitar.

'Man' (King/R. Gould/Badarou) 7:25

And so we come to the best track on *Staring* by quite some way. 'Man' is an ambitious mixed-meter piece with an intriguing ABA structure and some Mahavishnu Orchestra-style arpeggios in the refrain (first heard at 1:15), rapidly becoming a bit of a Mark trademark.

The first section makes the most of its basic D7/C7/G7 chord sequence, while the second features a brooding, ascending chord sequence, menacing spoken-word section, some excellent Mark bass and Krys Mach's powerful soprano sax. The third section cleverly returns to the opening chord sequence, this time with a swing feel. The simple 'Hey man/Sing the blues' refrain and excellent Alan Murphy guitar solo are a fitting ending to the track, and, frankly, it's a great relief to hear even such a vague reference to Black Music.

Boon's lyric plays ironically with the hippie ideal of 'man' as a term of endearment, widening out to become a gently self-admonishing portrait of good intentions going to waste.

'Man' was performed live throughout the *Staring* tour (and a decent live version appears on the streaming/Deluxe editions of the album), but one wonders what an audience expecting to hear 'Lessons In Love' and 'Something About You' thought of it.

'Gresham Blues' (King) 5:46

Named for the Dublin hotel where many of the *Staring* songs were written, this was one of the album's more successful tracks, a fine slice of blues-inflected jazz/rock in the vein of John McLaughlin's 'New York On My Mind' and 'The Unknown Dissident'. The melody and harmony lines are arresting while Mike, Alan Murphy and Krys Mach contribute excellent solos. Meanwhile, Gary delivers a superb performance, slowly building in intensity throughout the track until it sounds like he's ready to do some serious damage by the end (an interesting comparison is Simon Phillips's drum work on Nik Kershaw's 'Violet To Blue' from the British singer/guitarist/songwriter's 1986 album *Radio Musicola*). 'Gresham Blues' was an extra track on the original CD and cassette edition of *Staring*, not featuring on the vinyl version.

Extra tracks
'Three Words' (Lindup) 4:46

Stylistically, Mike's B-side to the 'Tracie' single is a definite precursor to his 1990 solo album *Changes*. It's a light, catchy but fairly anodyne pop/funk track with a nagging synth motif and on-the-nose lyrics. It has been added to the streaming/Deluxe versions of *Staring*.

Interlude: 1989

After the hugely successful *Staring At The Sun* tour wound up with a 26 January 1989 gig at the Brighton Centre, it was definitely time for a reset. Though the album hadn't quite met Polydor's sales expectations, Mark and Mike had been delighted with Gary and Alan Murphy's contributions, both musically and personally. It seemed as if there was a lot more to come from this new band configuration, though sadly, once again, dark clouds were settling on the horizon.

As February dawned, Mark's priority was to write and record a new single for inclusion on the upcoming *Level Best* greatest hits compilation. Mark, Mike, Gary and Alan gathered to lay down 'Take Care Of Yourself' at Mark's new home studio, dubbed The Summerhouse. It was a rare Mark solo composition, a fast half-time shuffle with a slick groove, slinky bassline and lots of catchy sections, if slightly lacking a killer hook. It was also a distinct move away from *Staring*'s 'rock' sensibility. Lyrically, it seemed to be a scathing attack on the policies of Prime Minister Margaret Thatcher ('Big T don't care/And you don't matter/Did she say where you'd have to stay/When the party`s over?').

Released as a single on 16 October 1989, 'Take Care Of Yourself' would prove to be Alan Murphy's final recording with the band (check out his great playing on the extended version, available on streaming versions of *Staring*) and Gary's debut playing an electronic drum kit – a performance which astonished Mark: 'He is a human machine. The guy is a phenomenon with tempo. Never shifts. "Take Care" was a first take'. The song also spawned the band's best video yet (sadly not featuring Murphy): a garish, expensive-looking trawl through the last 30 years of pop culture, with Mark, Mike and Gary hamming it up as Beatles lookalikes and burned-out hippies, including Gary's amusing tribute to the 1984 movie *This Is Spinal Tap*. But the video didn't do much for the song's success – it just scraped into the UK top 40, peaking at 39, Level's lowest chart placing since 1984.

At the outset of 1989, Mark and Mike had been unaware that Murphy was very unwell. In the early part of the year, the guitarist suddenly became gravely ill, and tragically died of AIDS-related pneumonia three days after the release of 'Take Care Of Yourself', on 19 October 1989. He was just 35 years old, and the band had lost a great friend and great guitarist: 'He was a tremendous player and a tremendous person. In the eighteen months we were friends, I learned so much from him about everything. When Al came in, he helped restore our confidence; it felt like a band again. And he had something to say musically and changed the band for the better', Mark told *Guitarist* magazine in 1991.

At the same time, Mark's marriage was splintering. In such trying times, it's hardly surprising that there was only minimal promotion for the *Level Best* compilation, released on 30 October 1989 and reaching a very healthy number 5 in the UK album charts. The band sabbatical gave Mike the chance to dust off some material he'd stockpiled during the first ten years of his career, and fashion it into a solo album. Polydor green-lighted the concept and work began on *Changes* in late 1989.

Changes (Mike Lindup solo) (1990)

Personnel:
Mike Lindup: Keyboards and Vocals
Dominic Miller: Guitars
Pino Palladino: Bass
Manu Katché: Drums
Miles Bould: Percussion
Danny Thompson: Acoustic Bass
Ann Morfee: Violin
Dave Heath: Flute
Carlos Fuentes: Percussion
German Santana: Percussion
Pato: Percussion
Calum Malcolm: Engineer
Hugh Padgham: Engineer
Calum Malcolm/Mike Lindup: Producers
Recorded at Metropolis Studios (London), Castlehouse (Edinburgh), February-April 1990.
Released: June 1990
Chart position: UK: –, US: –
Current edition: 2020 Knapdale Records, limited-edition vinyl

The Quiet One Speaks. In Mike's typically understated words, *Changes* 'presented an opportunity to put myself on the map as an artist in my own right'. Of course, there were already the solo compositions on Level albums – 'Woman', 'People' and 'Silence' – but there was a lot more to him than those tunes.

Changes also gave Mike the opportunity to work with a different group of musicians outside the Level 42 day job, and the band's reputation guaranteed him a first-rate rhythm section: Pino Palladino was possibly the most-recorded session bassist of the 1980s, famous for his work with Paul Young, Gary Numan, Tears For Fears, Joan Armatrading and Chris De Burgh; drummer Manu Katché (who reportedly completed his *Changes* tracks in just three days) had manned the sticks on Peter Gabriel's *So*, Sting's *...Nothing Like The Sun* and Joni Mitchell's *Chalk Mark In A Rainstorm*; guitarist Dominic Miller was retained from the *Staring* sessions; and percussionist Miles Bould had recently recorded and toured with Julia Fordham and John Martyn. Legendary acoustic bassist Danny Thompson – famous for his work with Martyn, David Sylvian, Pentangle and tens of other highly respected artists – also guested on one track.

Mike also assembled an esteemed back-room duo: co-producer Calum Malcolm was best known for his collaborations with The Blue Nile and Simple Minds, while superstar mixing engineer/producer Hugh Padgham (XTC, Peter Gabriel, David Bowie, Genesis, The Police) was brought in to work on *Changes*' title track and 'The Spirit Is Free'. Recorded at Castlesound in Edinburgh and Metropolis in Chiswick, West London, the album was also blessed with a striking cover, cooked up by the Bill Price studio who had worked their magic on collections by Toyah, The Jam, Kate Bush, Genesis, King Crimson and Steve Winwood.

Sadly, *Changes* was rather sidelined on its initial release, unable to build up any sales momentum which might have come its way had 'The Spirit Is Free' become a hit. It also received very limited promotion, with just a few advertisements in the glossy music monthlies. But the album is ripe for reappraisal and, at the time of writing, sounds extremely fresh, with strong melodies, uplifting grooves and a sumptuous mix. In October 2020, Mike announced that he was now in possession of the master tapes and would be releasing a 30th-anniversary vinyl edition, also revealing that he was working on *Changes II*.

'Changes' (Lindup) 6:20

It's a striking introduction to a solo career: an *a cappella* version of Jan Struther and Ralph Vaughan Williams' children's hymn 'When A Knight Won His Spurs', with some strikingly low notes from Mike. The rest of the song is excellent too, with an uplifting chorus, super-tight groove from Katché, very Mark-like bassline and a lovely modulation after the second chorus. The almost painfully-honest lyric subtly equates personal rebirth with political change, including the memorable line: 'It's clear the status quo is the first thing that must go'. Somewhat surprisingly, 'Changes' was not released as a single, but certainly benefits from Padgham's pristine mix.

'Lovely Day' (Lindup) 4:26

This is a slight but catchy piece which almost feels like Mike's anthem, perfectly chiming with his chipper public image: 'It's a lovely day today/I'm smiling like I usually do'. The song showcases a pleasingly minimalist arrangement: just Katché's soft reggae/funk groove, Miller's ambient effects, Mike's synths and a charming contribution from violinist Ann Morfee. She was Mike's contemporary at Chetham's school; 'Lovely Day' was her first professional recording session, though she would go on to a fine career including a spell in Michael Nyman's acclaimed ensemble. Better than almost anything on *Staring At The Sun*, 'Lovely Day' is likeable and uplifting, if a little leaden at times.

'Fallen Angel' (Lindup) 6:14

The opening, broken chords (F-maj7/E-min) are instantly recognisable as Mike's sound world. Lyrically, the nostalgia for a lost love is also very much his forte. Miller provides impressive acoustic guitar, Katché adds some clever, military-style snare drum and there's strong conga work from Bould. Though it lacks a catchy melody, 'Fallen Angel' hangs together very well thanks to some arresting arrangements such as the unexpected modulation at 3:24.

'The Spirit Is Free' (Lindup) 4:48

The only single released from *Changes*, this is a very impressive composition, if naggingly reminiscent of Shakatak's 1983 hit 'Dark Is The Night'. Mike delivers a strong vocal throughout in full 'chest' voice. He shows his arranging prowess too, with an unexpected pre-chorus section after the second verse. Miller gets his first two guitar solos of the album, drenched in reverb, the bluesy second one particularly effective. Lyrically, it's a typically empathetic song about escaping one's own romantic, political, economic or racial boundaries using freedom of thought and a positive outlook. It may also reflect Mike's interest in the Swiss psychiatrist/psychoanalyst Carl Jung. Inexplicably, 'The Spirit Is Free' didn't chart – a shame since it wasn't dissimilar to the kind of 'adult', sophisticated pop music that Sting was making at the time. An excellent version was performed throughout Level's *Guaranteed* tour, available to watch on the *Guaranteed Live* DVD.

'Desire' (Lindup) 4:38

The excellent 'Desire' sees the return of Mike's celebrated falsetto, and he also peppers the track with interesting arrangements such as the unexpected key change into the chorus. Miller's octave rhythm guitar features strongly in the right channel and he also contributes an effective, clean-toned Strat solo. Lyrically, the song is another painfully-honest – though never cloying – portrait of unrequited love, but, in typical Mike fashion, with a prevailing positivity.

'West Coast Man' (Lindup) 4:37

This was an agreeable shift to a mainly acoustic sound for Mike – 'West Coast Man' is a light and frothy track with a strong Brazilian influence courtesy of its gentle samba groove. There's an excellent contribution from Dave Heath on flute, who attended the Guildhall School of Music with Mike in the late 1970s. Miller layers acoustic guitars to fine effect, and we hear Palladino's fretless bass for the first time on *Changes*. Katché delivers a great performance, full of colour and drive, and Mike's vocal also has a lot of vitality.

'Judgement Day' (Lindup) 5:44

One of *Changes*' standouts, this is a really strong song with lots of good ideas and a great bassline. Bould's bongos, shaker and cowbell feature prominently, and Katché delivers another fine performance including a stunning fill at 1:36. Mike excels with a great array of keyboard sounds including a killer synth bass, sampled xylophone and layered synth pads. Lyrically, 'Judgement Day' seems to follow on from Level's 'Take Care Of Yourself': a very on-the-nose protest against Margaret Thatcher's policies ('How do you get through the day/When all around you ministers are saying they have had enough?').

'Life Will Never Be The Same' (Lindup) 4:41

This is an excellent, affecting ballad, beautifully sung and performed. It's a spiritual song, balancing the passing of time and ageing of loved ones against the universal power of love. Musically it's fairly simple, featuring just Mike's piano and voice, a few keyboard overdubs and Danny Thompson's inimitable acoustic bass. Though no trumpeter is listed on the album credits, it sounds uncannily like Mark Isham, the esteemed American solo artist and soundtrack composer.

'Paixão (Passion)' (Lindup) 5:40

Mike dips into his love of Brazilian music again here, enhancing 'Paixão' with a samba-school rhythm section consisting of Bould, Carlos Fuentes, German Santana and Pato. There's very prominent *cuica* and tambourine, and Mark delivers an excellent vocal performance with an impressive range. It's possibly the weakest song on *Changes*, but still enjoyable due to its arrangement, attractive middle-eight and superb production.

'Jung' (Lindup) 6:56

Palladino makes his second and final *Changes* appearance on this fine instrumental closer, kicking off with a nice run of harmonics. The first minute of the track is very much in a 'soundtrack' style, foregrounding Mike's moody synths and Miller's ambient stylings. It builds to become somewhat of a rock instrumental, and Miller closes with a strong, bluesy solo, very much in a Dave Gilmour style. 'Jung' makes for a likeable though hardly essential closer to *Changes* – a selection of pleasing textures and chord changes without much of a through line.

Guaranteed (1991)

Personnel:
Mark King: Bass and Vocals
Mike Lindup: Keyboards and Vocals
Gary Husband: Drums, Vocals and Keyboards
Wally Badarou: Keyboards and Vocals
Annie McCaig: Vocals
Allan Holdsworth: Guitar
Dominic Miller: Guitar
Gary Barnacle: Saxophone
John Thirkell: Trumpet
Record Label: RCA
Recorded: The Summerhouse (Isle Of Wight), June-September 1990
Released: October 1991
Running Time: 57:46
Highest Chart Placing: UK: 3, US: –
Current edition: 2009 Edsel with bonus tracks

After Mike had wrapped up work on *Changes*, Mark, Mike, Gary, guitarist
Dominic Miller and the new John Thirkell/Gary Barnacle horn section
convened at Mark's house in the early summer of 1990 to begin work on
Guaranteed, Level 42's ninth studio album. But this time around, there was a
slightly more muted feel to things; it was almost as if the band was starting all
over again. They hadn't played live for eighteen months and were still reeling
from the death of Alan Murphy. It was also a time of personal upheaval for
Mark: he was dealing with the breakup of his first marriage and had just turned
30. 'Because I was going through a lot of grief, it made the album even more
precious to me', Mark told *Q Magazine*'s Stuart Maconie in 1994.

He channelled his energies into a batch of new compositions, laying down
the demos using an Akai/Linn MPC60 workstation and drum sampler. He told
Making Music's Paul Tingen about his songwriting processes around this time:

The key word is inspiration. Some days you've got it and others you haven't.
Hell, I don't know where these notes come from. They spring into my head
and I sing them through and then usually forget them. But the next day I
might be singing it again and stick it down in the studio and that's where it
starts unravelling itself. The song takes shape in front of you. When I arrange, I
only record the backbeat on the MPC60. If the melody is strong enough, it will
hold. I just 'la-la-la' through it and start work on the lyrics later on, or give an
idea in that form to one of the people who write lyrics for us.

Mark was alluding to a new songwriting process with which he and Mike were
experimenting: for the first time in the band's history, they were attempting to
compose music to a pre-existing set of words. Though, famously, Elton John

worked that way in collaboration with lyricist Bernie Taupin, it was certainly not the 'standard' songwriting procedure. But with Boon not available for *Guaranteed*, it was a good opportunity to try out some new wordsmiths. One was Nashville-based George Green, who had also previously collaborated with his childhood friend John 'Cougar' Mellencamp on US hits such as 'Crumblin' Down' and 'Hurts So Good'. The American flavour of Green's work pulled Mark in a new direction too, 'My Father's Shoes' in particular emerging with a distinctly country and western vibe. Another new lyricist was Drew Barfield, one-time bassist and vocalist with A&M-signed, early-1980s pop contenders The Keys, and writer for Joe Jackson, Go West and Paul Young (with whom he later performed in covers band Los Pacaminos).

Mark was also expanding his bass repertoire, 'hearing' different tones for the new album. As a result, he used a Music Man Stingray five-string bass on two tracks, a fretless on another. In the guitar department, Mark and Miller contributed rhythm parts, but then the former had a brainwave as the album sessions were coming to the end: would Allan Holdsworth, Gary's trusted friend and collaborator, come onboard to play some solos? Incredibly, the answer came back in the affirmative. This was unprecedented: Holdsworth was a very occasional and mostly reluctant guest on other artists' material. Mark was thrilled to have him onboard: 'He did us a big favour. I never thought he'd lower himself to come and play with us, but the guy was fantastic! He'd been a hero of ours. It felt right that the guy who filled Al Murphy's shoes was the guy that Al always thought was the dog's bollocks!', he told *Guitarist* magazine. Gary explained a little more about the process of getting Allan involved:

As I remember, it all happened pretty quickly. Towards the end of our recording sessions for *Guaranteed*, Mark suddenly had the idea to invite Allan, primarily as a soloist. I, of course, had a direct link to him and Allan responded very enthusiastically. As far as my memory recalls, he seemed to make it over to the Isle Of Wight quite quickly, and in no time was performing not only those wonderful, yearning solos in all the spots required, but falling back and playing rhythm parts also, which really blew me away. Allan, you have to understand, not only did not ever involve himself in conventional rhythm guitar-playing, but pretty much disliked it. In spite of that, he turned in magnificent, absolutely majestic performances. Mark was overjoyed – everybody was! Me particularly.

Allan's arrival was a huge boost to the band, and consequently there was a great sense of optimism around the final recording sessions for *Guaranteed*. But a big shock was in store: when they presented the album to Polydor in September 1990, the label refused to release it, believing there weren't enough hit singles. It was a pretty shocking *volte-face* from a label who just three years earlier had seen their charges release a seven-million-selling record. But Polydor also had some form in this department: the same thing had happened to The Style Council a year earlier when the band's fifth studio collection *Modernism: A New Decade* was deemed unreleasable by the label. Enough was enough for Mark, Mike and Paul Crockford: rather than spend another six months re-recording and/or writing new songs, they quickly found a new deal with RCA Records and *Guaranteed* was scheduled for autumn 1991.

In the meantime, they turned their attentions to live performance. Back in December 1988, anticipating their impending sabbatical, they had booked the Hammersmith Odeon for fifteen nights (apparently breaking Elton John's record of fourteen) between 5-22 December 1990. As the gigs fast approached, the immediate concern was who would play guitar. Mark and Gary had assumed that Holdsworth wouldn't want to stick around after the *Guaranteed* sessions, so asked him to recommend a successor. To everyone's surprise and delight, Allan volunteered for the Hammersmith concerts. Gary takes up the story:

Mark wanted to investigate into whether Allan would fancy coming on the road for a short tour, but playing the band's set at that time, with a sprinkle of *Guaranteed* songs. Allan was as high as a kite from the enjoyable experience of the recording sessions, but I had to warn him he'd be expected to learn all Boon's work on the early recordings – doubling basslines and other rhythmic aspects – and I was a little worried. To my amazement, Allan wanted to really woodshed it and work hard. Mark offloaded eight or so CDs for Allan to prep, and again, to my astonishment, he applied himself really well with all the old material, playing all the parts faithfully and authentically. I think Allan had a lot of respect for Mark. I have so much respect for Mark. There's something about him, and the gentleman he is, where you can't not want to work hard for him! That said, I was really amazed at Allan's application and work ethic – especially for that brief tour. He really did great!

Drawing approximately 52,000 visitors, the Hammersmith shows also featured sessionman Lyndon Connah (George Michael, Squeeze, Swing Out Sister) on keyboards, alongside the Barnacle/Thirkell horn section and Annie McCaig on vocals. The concerts were a triumph. Holdsworth delivered some mind-bending solos, the Mark/Gary rhythm section was on fire, and the band garnered some of the best live reviews of their career.

In early 1991, at the suggestion of RCA, esteemed New York mixing engineer Tom Lord-Alge (Steve Winwood, Chaka Khan, Jeff Beck, Earth, Wind & Fire) sprinkled his fairy dust onto the *Guaranteed* tracks, adding some real sonic heft for the American market. But Gary in particular now has some reservations about this decision:

The original, rough mixes were done by Mark and Wally. As far as I'm concerned, they were the definitive mixes of the record. It was a great, great job. The tracks sounded wonderful to me – tight, dry, punchy and very funky. What the mixing engineer in New York ended up bringing to the album – masses of FM-radio compression, etc. – sounded in comparison quite disappointing to me. But there seemed to be pressure to use this engineer since he was thought of as the 'happening guy' of the moment.

Unsurprisingly, Holdsworth couldn't commit to any more live dates after the Hammersmith concerts, so Mark recruited guitarist Jakko Jakszyk, best known for his session work with Tom Robinson, Swing Out Sister and Sam Brown, as well as a short-lived solo career with Stiff Records in the early 1980s. Mark had received a tape from Jakko around 1988 and also spotted him playing with Robinson on *The James Whale Radio Show*: 'I was really impressed because I understand what it's like playing live on television', Mark later told *Guitarist* magazine. Jakszyk was swiftly recruited for the *Guaranteed* cover photo, and also appeared on a few B-sides, hastily recorded at Mark's studio during spring 1991.

Guaranteed was finally released in October. As usual, it was a solid success in the UK, reaching number 3 in the album charts and earning silver status, and also in the Netherlands. But a memorable, merciless *NME* review summed up just how passé the band now seemed to the British music press: 'There's a newly-wed van driver, right now, delivering office equipment in Milton Keynes, for whom the new Level 42 album means a great deal. One pictures Mark King behind security cameras inside his newly completed studio on the Isle Of Wight, churning out endless suburban-opiate muzak for Tories everywhere, and one vomits'! *Q Magazine* were also unimpressed, saying that the album featured 'Mark King's limited voice over bland jazz/funk workouts', but reckoned 'If You Were Mine' could be 'a pointer for the future'.

But *Guaranteed* was certainly an artistic success: though a little overlong, it played to the band's strengths of melody, groove and virtuosity. It was a big improvement on *Staring At The Sun*, lighter in touch, and with much more musical variety. The sober, black-and-white album cover screams 'grown-up album', but was actually quite misleading; it's a very 'up' record, but also distinctly the end of an era for the band, and, in some ways, also the end for this kind of mature, musicianly, well-produced 'pop'.

'Guaranteed' (Lindup/Badarou/King/Husband) 4:53

Released in August 1991, *Guaranteed*'s lead-off single reached number 17 in the UK. It also cracked the top 20 in Holland and Belgium and was arguably their strongest seven-incher since 'Children Say'. With its chugging bassline and galloping rhythm, it was a conscious nod to 'Lessons In Love', and also marked Allan Holdsworth's recording debut with the band, even if he was restricted to playing power chords during the verses. Gary makes his presence felt here as songwriter and multi-instrumentalist, providing lyrics, keyboards and coming up with the music for the excellent middle-eight. All in all, 'Guaranteed' is an effective distillation of the classic Level sound, and was played live throughout 1991.

'Overtime' (Lindup/King/Barfield) 4:46

Released as the album's second single in October 1991, the excellent
'Overtime' reached a lowly 62 in the UK singles chart, their lowest position for
six years. That's a shame because it's another fine pop song, musically rich with
a great keyboard hook line, clever modal verse melody and superb middle-
eight with fine backing vocals from Annie McCaig. Dominic Miller adds strong
rhythm guitar in the left channel and Gary Barnacle plays a full-bodied tenor
solo with a hint of Norwegian jazz great Jan Garbarek.

Once again, this uplifting song puts the bleakness of *Staring At The Sun*
further into the past. The video, shot in black-and-white, was a bit of a
misstep: a *Carry On*-style romp featuring Mark, Jakko and Gary as factory
workers (of course Mark falls for the blonde tea lady and has to put in some
'overtime'...) and Mike as the prissy quality-control inspector, complete with
glasses, overcoat and clipboard. You get the picture. Mark's occasionally-
remarked-upon resemblance to British actor Robin Askwith – star of the 1970s
Confessions films – seems apt here.

'Her Big Day' (Lindup/Badarou/King/Husband/Barfield) 5:08

There are surprisingly few 'pop' songs about the marriage ceremony: Elton
John's 'Kiss The Bride', Sting's 'The Secret Marriage', XTC's 'Big Day' and The
Dixie Cups' 'Chapel Of Love' come to mind. This was Level's contribution, a
band composition based on Barfield's lyrics – a neat, sometimes witty summary
of a bride and groom's internal thoughts. Gary's snare drum is beefed up
with a trigger effect and he was gainfully employed from the keyboard chair,
contributing the Herbie Hancock-ish motif at 2:47 and a short acoustic piano
solo. The vocal and horn arrangements are winning and the band generally
throw everything but the kitchen sink into this track, even adding a little
impression of the Bow Bells at 2:39.

Essentially just a jam in A with various licks and tricks, 'Her Big Day' is a fairly
slight but likeable tune, played live throughout 1991.

'Seven Years' (King) 4:43

This was only Mark's second solo credit on a Level 42 song, and was, on the
surface at least, a very personal track touching on the breakup of his marriage –
almost the flip side of the band's earlier 'Seven Days'. It's also intriguing in that
it seems to be directed at the newly-single divorcee, with some striking lines:
'Baby's gone/Now what are you gonna do/Was there ever a day/Just one day
you were happy'.

The song is also notable for featuring Mark on fretless bass for the first time
on a Level 42 album. 'I did the old thing of hooking some frets out of the bass,
shoving in the wood filler and voila! – a fretless bass. Not a particularly great
one, but it wouldn't make any difference to me, because it's so different', he
told *Guitarist* magazine in 1991. He uses it to great effect here, coming up
with a lovely countermelody during the instrumental introduction. Dominic

Miller and Allan Holdsworth share guitar duties – Miller plays a twelve-string acoustic, while Holdsworth contributes two gorgeous electric solos, the first aping Mark's bass melody (at 2:59). Annie McCaig also makes the first of many key contributions on vocals, meshing seamlessly with Mike and Mark during the chorus and refrain. At the time of writing, the impressive 'Seven Years' has yet to be performed live.

'Set Me Up' (Lindup/King/Barfield) 4:27

'Set Me Up' is the first track on *Guaranteed* that feels a little like 'Level by numbers'. Another groove in E – similar to *World Machine*'s 'Coup D'état' – it features some less-than-essential Mark bass and an almost non-existent chorus. But Mike delivers a powerful vocal, a nice pre-chorus section very reminiscent of his solo song 'Changes' then and an excellent keyboard interlude featuring a very Herbie Hancock-like chord change at 2:25. Gary's snare drum is the star of this song though – he plays some pile-driving stuff in the style of Billy Cobham. 'Set Me Up' is possibly the weakest track on *Guaranteed*, but still better than almost anything on *Staring*. At the time of writing, it has only been played in concert twice.

'The Ape' (King/Green) 4:15

'The Ape' is the other track on *Guaranteed* which is close to filler – it's only really notable for Mark's catchy, occasionally-doubled bassline, hitting some exceptionally low notes on his five-string, and Gary Barnacle's sprightly sax soloing throughout. Gary Husband also adds witty keyboards in the second half, including some pedal-steel guitar sounds at 2:36. 'The Ape' could easily have been left off *Guaranteed*, but it's a fairly harmless slice of jazzy pop/funk. At the time of writing, it has never been played live.

'My Father's Shoes' (Green/King/Lindup/Badarou) 5:12

Originally intended as a B-side or extra track, 'My Father's Shoes' finally made the cut for *Guaranteed* and even became its third and final single, reaching UK number 55 in April 1992. Musically and lyrically it's a real detour for the band, a 'story' song almost in a country and western vein. Mark's choice of bass for the track was an MB4 – a Wal fitted with a MIDI device, lending the tone a bendy, 'fretless' quality. Dominic Miller's acoustic and twelve-string Rickenbacker guitars feature strongly. Surprisingly, 'My Father's Shoes' was a big favourite of British radio presenter Danny Baker, occasionally played on his BBC London shows between 2001 and 2012. At the time of writing, it has never been played live.

'A Kinder Eye' (King/Green) 5:45

This arresting and ambitious track is one of *Guaranteed*'s standouts. Green's lyric, dedicated to his mother-in-law, is somewhat long-winded but features a few telling lines: 'Though he'd signed a thousand paintings/Still he'd never finished one'. It prompts a highly original verse melody from King, and also inspires some great band performances: Mike 'comps' through the first half of the opening verse on synth, but then Holdsworth takes over at 1:14, adding his trademark, close-interval voicings. In the second verse, Mike adds some pretty piano countermelodies, before Holdsworth embarks on a memorable solo. The last minute of the track features some terrific Husband/Holdsworth interplay. Inspired by Holdsworth's brilliance, 'A Kinder Eye' is a new kind of Level 42 song, sadly a direction not really subsequently explored. At the time of writing, it has yet to be performed live.

'She Can't Help Herself' (Lindup/King/Barfield) 5:00

This is another successful departure for the band, a slow ballad in 6/8 time, opening with Mark's harmonics and some tricky, over-the-bar-line triplets. 'She Can't Help Herself' also features more of Holdsworth's chordal brilliance, particularly between 0:08 and 0:30. He also plays two excellent solos: the first at 2:24 is accompanied by some tasty chord changes, while the second takes the tune out, ending brilliantly with a minor-third string bend. Barfield's lyric portrays a troubled young woman – with shades of Randy Newman's 'Real Emotional Girl' – and the gentle humanism of the final minute is touching ('Don't cry/Leave a light on the landing hall/Don't cry/There's a rainbow behind that door'). Again, it's not everyone's cup of tea, but 'She Can't Help Herself' is a fine composition if one can accept that the band are broadening their horizons. A demo version, featuring Mark on drums, appeared on the 2012 *Living It Up* box set. The song was performed live throughout 1991.

'If You Were Mine' (Husband) 5:01

'If You Were Mine' is another highlight of the band's 1990s output and yet another strong song on *Guaranteed*. It was performed live throughout 1991. Gary outlined the genesis of his composition:

> It was something I wrote specifically for the band. I knocked together a demo and Mark's reaction was that he was eager to go for it, which was very cool. One of my favourite 'up' songs from the original band was 'Fashion Fever', and I wanted to write something with that kind of immediacy, but it turned out that 'If You Were Mine' didn't evoke 'Fashion Fever' in the least! Nevertheless, it had a good spirit about it and even gave Allan and I the chance to get some interaction going towards the end. Mark sang it wonderfully and came up with the repeated horn motif in the end section, which gives way to the guitar-and-drums freak-out.

One element of 'If You Were Mine' which does resemble 'Fashion Fever' is the distinctive two-bar melody first heard at 0:15 (similar to the two-bar riff that kicks off 'Fashion Fever'). Mark's Stevie Wonder-style horn/vocal line is a real highlight, as is his bass-playing throughout, including a great descending lick at 3:28. It's also a nice touch to begin the song with an instrumental version of the middle-eight.

All in all, 'If You Were Mine' is a memorable, bombastic piece, with excellent vocals from Mark, Mike and McCaig, and a storming jazz/rock outro that couldn't have been played by any other 'pop' band during the 1990s: a source of great pride to Mark. Gary's lyric is also interesting, cleverly inverting the final line of each verse: 'I'm always the last to know you're trying to love me too/ You're always the last to know I'm trying to love you too'.

'Lasso The Moon' (Green/Lindup) 4:02

Mike confirmed his newfound confidence as a singer on this track which moves quite naturally into Sting territory, with its gentle bossa nova vibe and flowing melody. Gary Husband's snare-drum technique gets a great workout again, though his playing is at times a tad overbearing. Gary Barnacle's tenor sax solo also seems a little superfluous. Green's lyric is an interesting exploration of the masculine ideal of being a 'hero' and family breadwinner. The title is a reference to some key dialogue in Frank Capra's 1946 movie *It's A Wonderful Life,* when George (James Stewart) tells Mary (Donna Reed) about his dreams for the future. Deserving more attention, 'Lasso The Moon' is a strong song and one of Mike's key contributions to the band. At the time of writing, it hasn't been performed live.

'With A Little Love' (Husband/King) 4:08

Guaranteed closes with another memorable track, a musically-rich composition featuring some cracking rhythm-section playing (arguably the peak of the King/ Husband combination) and a lyric that manages to be sentimental without being cloying. Gary explained how the song came about:

'With A Little Love' was a (chord) sequence featuring that exact harmony and bassline movement I had knocking around at the time. I did the keyboards, including the overdriven, guitar-like Korg M1 solo. I'm using the same sound as the one much used on my *Diary Of A Plastic Box* album from 1989. Mark put the lyrics and melody line together.

It was a fine and fitting album-closer – a sophisticated, jazzy number with something for everyone. At the time of writing, 'With A Little Love' has yet to be played live.

Extra tracks
'All She Wants' (Lindup/Husband/King/Barfield) 4:14

The cheery B-side to the 'Guaranteed' single, 'All She Wants' very nearly made the final tracklisting for the album. But apart from Gary's exciting, barelycontainable playing, it's a very minor piece, with a few corny touches like the harmonised guitar/bass riff opening the second verse.

'At This Great Distance' (Green/King/Lindup) 4:45

This was a quietly ambitious B-side to the 'Overtime' single, also available on the two-CD *Guaranteed Deluxe Edition* released in 2009, and it marked Jakko's recording debut with the band. It's full of intriguing moments: Mark's harmonic run and spoken-word sections, Mike's glacial synths, more McLaughlin guitar arpeggios and some of the most 'rock' playing from the band thus far. Gary is also really in his element during the second half, unleashing some cracking fusion chops.

'As Years Go By' (Green/King) 4:37

A very rare shuffle from the band, this impressive B-side also featured Jakko on guitar and some strong horn section work from John Thirkell and Gary Barnacle. It's an excellent song with a very catchy pre-chorus section, and is well worth seeking out.

Interlude: 1992-1994

The band toured the UK and Europe extensively throughout 1991 and 1992, playing a lot of material from *Guaranteed* and showcasing perhaps the most impressive vocals of any Level 42 line-up, with Annie McCaig and Jakko perfectly complimenting Mark and Mike. The live dates included two outdoor concerts at London's Crystal Palace Bowl and a filmed performance at the same city's Town & Country Club on 20 March 1992, later released on video as *Guaranteed Live* (see below).

Gary Husband left the band for the first time in the spring of 1992, returning briefly to a prestigious career as sideman to the likes of Allan Holdsworth, Jack Bruce and Billy Cobham. But he has no regrets about his initial five-year spell with Level 42, and remains proud of his contribution to *Guaranteed*:

> On the writing front, it was great to have the opportunity to bring in 'If You Were Mine' and 'With A Little Love'. I was also very happy to be getting creatively involved in keyboard ideas, as well as little collaborative writing additions to certain other songs. Mark always so kindly extended an invitation to get as hands-on as possible, and that was both great of him and very fulfilling for me.

Gary also feels that the band had achieved all they set out to during those initial post-Phil-and-Boon years:

> As far as whether that particular direction had reached its conclusion or not, I think it had. All recordings represent a stepping stone of some kind or another; *Guaranteed* was a far-reaching album, with a lot of diversity. I'm happy that it came out in accordance with how Mark, Mike and Wally intended it.

But Gary was also a close witness to the commercial pressures Mark and Mike were sometimes put under in terms of producing 'relevant' contemporary material that could compete with the band's past work:

> There did seem to be one hell of a lot of ever-present record company criteria for the band to be producing material that was in line with the trends of that time. Level 42 had their direction and had established their own footing from the start, and on their own terms. I feel Mark and Mike should have been granted more provision as to how they felt they could integrate the changing trends into their music. They'd proved themselves and stuck to their guns. That's certainly not in question.

Forever Now (1994)

Personnel:
Mark King: Bass, Organ, Loops, Harp and Lead Vocals
Mike Lindup: Synthesizer, Fender Rhodes, Grand Piano, Wurlitzer, Hammond XB2 and Vocals
Phil Gould: Drums, Acoustic Piano, Drum Loops, Organ and Vocals
Danny Blume: Guitar
Wally Badarou: Vocals, Synths, Guitars, Yamaha DX7, Fender Rhodes and Hammond XB2
Miles Bould: Percussion
Mitey: Vocals
Gary Barnacle: Saxophones
John Thirkell: Trumpet
Derek Watkins: Trumpet
Stuart Brooks: Trumpet
Richard Edwards: Trombone
Producers: Level 42, Steve Anderson and Wally Badarou
Engineer: Steve Fitzmaurice
Record Label: RCA
Recorded: The Summerhouse (Isle Of Wight), Swanyard (London), Sarm West (London), Marcus (London), Winter 1993
Released: 14 March 1994
Running Time: 51:59
Highest Chart Placing: UK: 8, US: –
Current edition: 2009 Edsel with bonus tracks

The death of Alan Murphy, ending of Mark's first marriage and the band's split with Polydor had made Mark a lot more philosophical as 1992 turned into 1993. It was a time to let bygones be bygones, to reacquaint with old friends; it was time to reunite with his old pal Phil. 'When you stand at one of your best mate's deathbeds, you realise you shouldn't get hung up on being right or wrong. I hadn't seen Phil since he left in 1987, but after five years I started to remember what great pals we'd been and what good times we'd had. I called him up and he felt pretty much the same', Mark told *Q Magazine* in 1994.

He was also very much becoming a homebody again, enjoying his return to the Isle Of Wight. 'Family's very important to me. I'm very close to my mum and dad, brothers and sisters, and they're all on the island', Mark told *Making Music*'s Paul Tingen. He had also embarked on a new relationship and bought a bar in Ryde, calling it Joe DaFlo's – a mash-up of his children's names.

The reunion with Phil resulted in quite a brave and unexpected Level 42 album, and the creation of a new hybrid sound for the band. *Forever Now*, recorded again mainly at Mark's Summerhouse home studio, was to some extent influenced by the neo-jazz/funk sound made popular in the early 1990s by artists such as The Brand New Heavies, Omar and Galliano. Ironically, all were to some extent influenced by the original Britfunk bands, so things really had come full circle.

The new Level sound was relatively sparse, with more of a 'live' feel and very few sequencers, samples or synths. Mark's bass tone was 'fatter' than ever before, Phil's drum parts very minimalistic and lo-fi, and the arrangements and production generally unadorned. The song was paramount, instrumental virtuosity very much kept in check. Mike dusted off his Fender Rhodes and also provided some excellent string arrangements. Co-producer Wally was taking on a more varied musical role, adding a few background vocals and even a few guitar parts alongside his keyboards. Gary Barnacle and John Thirkell were joined by some extra horn players, and there were also two new names in the rhythm section: percussionist Miles Bould – recommended by Mike after the *Changes* sessions – and American session guitarist Danny Blume.

But between 1991 and 1994, the chart landscape had shifted, and once again it seemed that Level's timing was unfortunate – guitar-based Britpop was building up a head of steam and 'manufactured pop' was again coming very much to the fore. According to Mike, RCA's A&R department was very hands-on with *Forever Now*, advising on song structures and potential singles (and asking dance duo K-Klass to remix a few tracks). But then the label seemed to disappear when it came to promoting the album, the newly-signed Take That apparently demanding most of their attention.

The writing sessions were certainly fruitful though, and once again the band would have a huge pool of material to choose from: 22 songs were considered for the album. Tracks that didn't make the cut were eventually released via special versions for the Japanese market and also a 1995 two-CD reissue. Phil was drawing on a rich seam of inspiration for his lyrics, conjuring some highly original takes on the love song and also taking on the mid-90s 'crisis in masculinity'. There was even some self-mocking 1980s-baiting thrown in for good measure.

Flawed but full of great moments and memorable tunes, *Forever Now* is a fascinating reboot, ripe for reassessment, and at its best when it steers clear of the funk – something you don't often say about Level. Curiously, at the time of writing, it's not available on streaming platforms in its original form.

'Forever Now' (Frank Musker/Richard Darbyshire/King) 4:14

This was a very bold statement of intent for the new Level, a change of musical direction pitched somewhere between The Brand New Heavies and Swing Out Sister. Written by Mark alongside Living In A Box mainman Richard Darbyshire and Lisa Stansfield/Brian May/Bucks Fizz collaborator Frank Musker, the song is either irresistibly upbeat or irritatingly jaunty, depending on your disposition. The in-your-face production was certainly a big shock in comparison to *Guaranteed*, as was the prevalence of horns and wah-wah rhythm guitar.

Released in February 1994 as the album's lead-off single, 'Forever Now' made number 8 in the UK but was not a hit in Europe, much to Mike's chagrin. He also reported (in *The Very Best Of Level 42* liner notes) that the lyric concept was inspired by Stephen Hawking's famous 1988 book *A Brief History Of Time*. If so, they were in good company, Frank Zappa apparently also being similarly smitten by Hawking's concepts in the late 80s.

An interesting demo of 'Forever Now' has appeared on YouTube, featuring a more patently Latin groove and Mark's chant ('We got twenty thousand million years/Then the whole damn thing disappears') becoming a major part of the track. The song was performed live throughout 1994, making a brief comeback in 2016.

'Model Friend' (King/Lindup/P. Gould) 4:56

Phil's crisp snare drum ushers in a catchy but lightweight tune, featuring yet another great Mark bassline. But unfortunately 'Model Friend' lacks a memorable chorus and seriously outstays its welcome, sticking around for about a minute too long. The most interesting thing about the song is the lyric, something you don't often say about Level – the protagonist is a so-called 'new man' trying not to focus on how much he is physically attracted to his female friend, and wondering what the future holds for such 'unreconstructed', heterosexual males. At the time of writing, it's both witty and relevant. 'Model Friend' was played live occasionally during 1994.

'Tired Of Waiting' (Lindup/Badarou/P. Gould) 4:57

One of *Forever Now's* highlights, 'Tired Of Waiting' is another of those catchy, upbeat but still musically rich songs that the band does so well. The presence of Wally's name in the songwriting credits surely contributes to that. Mike's Fender Rhodes makes a welcome return, Mark gets a big bass tone with his Music Man Stingray and Phil lays down a sprightly two-step groove with a refreshingly different feel to a lot of the band's material. At the time of writing, 'Tired Of Waiting' has yet to be played live.

'All Over You' (King/Lindup/P. Gould) 4:01

Released as *Forever Now's* second single in April 1994, 'All Over You' reached number 26 in the UK. With its propulsive bassline, crisp snare drum and staccato horns, it can't help but bring to mind 'Hot Water'. But it's also weirdly out of sync with the rest of *Forever Now* and lacks the really decent melody and chorus melodies that grace the classic Level singles. The lyric and title's double entendres are fairly unsubtle, but there are still pleasures to be found, particularly the opening Mahavishnu-style arpeggios and Phil's subtle snare rolls and hi-hat barks.

An interesting demo version has appeared on YouTube featuring Mike singing lead, an added spoken-word section, and a far busier drum performance from Phil. 'All Over You' was played live throughout 1994 and has resurfaced occasionally since.

'Love In A Peaceful World' (P. Gould/Steve White) 7:24

Released as the third single from album in August 1994, 'Love In A Peaceful World' reached 31 in the UK – presumably somewhat of a disappointment as it's a very strong song with a touch of Hall & Oates about it. The band's last UK top 40 single to date, it was a collaboration between Phil and his good friend and Style Council/Paul Weller drummer Steve White. The track dated from 1992, when Phil laid down a demo with Galliano/Jamiroquai vocalist Valerie Etienne for a mooted solo project which never saw the light of day.

The lyric is simple and direct, a potent plea for unity, extrapolating from the personal to the political. Vocally, the song is also impressive, with Mark's emotive performance and Mike's triple-tracked chorus both soothing and excellently rendered. His fine string arrangement is played by a section including esteemed violinist Gavin Wright.

A little-seen video was made featuring British session drummer Frank Tontoh manning the skins. Frank also joined the band during promotional appearances for the song. 'Love In A Peaceful World' was occasionally played live during 1994.

'Romance' (King/Lindup/P. Gould) 4:55

This makes a successful left-turn into Leon Ware/Marvin Gaye territory – circa the latter's *I Want You* – a slow-burning, funky ballad with gorgeous chord harmony (including a crucial change of outlook at 3:30), one of Mark's most heartfelt vocal performances, and a very catchy Mike refrain. Mike's string chart is also excellent, with echoes of the great Motown arranger Paul Riser, and Miles Bould's fine conga-playing is high in the mix.

Lyrically, the song also impresses, with one of the best opening lines in the Level catalogue: 'Away with all those tales of romance', the cry of the lovelorn everywhere. 'Romance' has only been played live once at the time of writing, at London's Metropolis Studios on 10 December 2011 (available to watch on the *Live From Metropolis Studios* DVD).

'Billy's Gone' (King/P. Gould) 5:25

Featuring a 24-carat groove in the classic Level style, the impressive 'Billy's Gone' was written at only Mark and Phil's second meeting since 1987. 'It sounds quite fresh and emotional', Mark told *Q Magazine*'s Stuart Maconie in 1994. The verse melody and harmony hint at a James Taylor influence. There's some great gospel-inspired piano from Mike while Mark delivers a powerful, uncharacteristically raw vocal, especially during the heartfelt middle section ('And as a matter of fact/I'm not taking you back'). Phil's snare drum has never been crisper or higher in the mix. His lyrics are excellent too: it's a subtle love song from the perspective of a potential suitor who may or may not be trying to resuscitate an old relationship. We end with Mark's (sampled?) low vocals, sounding uncannily like a didgeridoo. Somewhat of an undiscovered gem, 'Billy's Gone' has never been performed live at the time of writing.

'One In A Million' (King/Lindup/Badarou/P. Gould) 4:28

Featuring a rare half-time shuffle in the style of 'Freedom Someday', 'One In A Million' is the classic-single-that-never-was and arguably Mike's finest hour in the band; Stevie Wonder would have been happy to write this. It's a deceptively breezy song about loneliness and the search for a life partner. There's also a beguiling instrumental middle-eight and a cool key change into the final chorus at 3:26, a Mike trademark. Mark's bass work is perfectly tasteful and doesn't do anything to distract from the vocals. Sumptuously arranged and performed, 'One In A Million' is an underrated gem, definitely due a reappraisal. It was performed occasionally on the 1994 UK tour.

'The Sunbed Song' (King/P. Gould) 5:17

This is one song that needs to be listened to right through to the end. It's a typically likeable if hardly remarkable piece for four minutes, with great Phil drums and trademark lyrics ('Won't even try to justify my sunglasses'!), and there's even Mike's homage to 'Turn It On'. But the track suddenly concludes with a stunning Mahavishnu-style jazz/rock breakdown, complete with Phil's Cobham-esque snare work and Danny Blume's scary wah-wah guitar solo which had me scanning the liner notes to see if Mr. McLaughlin had made a rare guest appearance. 'The Sunbed Song' made its live debut in 2001, and has appeared occasionally in setlists ever since.

'Talking In Your Sleep' (King/Lindup/P. Gould) 3:46

This is one of *Forever Now's* simplest and most effective songs, with a superb, uncharacteristically gentle vocal by King, and a great chorus. It sounds like Phil has dusted off one of his 1980s snare drums, and Mike's Rhodes solo works perfectly, as does Wally's Hammond organ. Mike's subtle string arrangement enhances the second verse, followed by a great outro featuring Jan Hammer-style vintage-synth licks and a beatific vocal motif. Phil contributes a fine lyric, the protagonist slowly realising that his partner is having an affair, summoning some excellent metaphors:

> Like the way that it looks in a seaside town
> When the shutters go up and the flags come down
> And the beaches are bare
> No one around
> That's me today

At the time of writing, the intimate 'Talking In Your Sleep' has never been performed live.

'Don't Bother Me' (King/P. Gould) 4:50

Forever Now rather shudders to a halt with this underwhelming closer which probably could have been left on the cutting-room floor. The song is based around a fairly hackneyed acoustic guitar riff which quickly outstays its welcome, but it does rally for an interesting, memorable chorus. Bould contributes some excellent percussion, while Phil's lyric is world-weary and possibly Mark-baiting:

Spent the 80s in a trance
Led us on a merry dance
You were always advocating power games
You were always gonna be a star
You made your money
Had your fun
Made a video about how it's done

Ouch! At the time of writing, 'Don't Bother Me' has yet to be played live.

Extra tracks
'Past Lives' (King/P. Gould) 5:35
World Machine/Running In The Family veteran Julian Mendelsohn was on mixing and engineering duties for this 'Forever Now' B-side which also appeared on the 2007 *Best Of The RCA Years* compilation. It kicks off with a rehash of Mark's bassline from the *A Physical Presence* version of '88' – though in a different key (B rather than E) – with some great Bould congas and lovely panoramic keyboard sounds from Mike. The catchy chorus has a nice reggae feel and chords very reminiscent of Stevie Wonder's 'Master Blaster (Jammin')'. The funny spoken-word section compares the narrator's realisation that he's in a cycle of romantic disappointments to a horror movie: 'Welcome to the house of Usher'! But Mike's soothing Fender Rhodes solo says that everything will turn out OK. It's good to hear the band letting their hair down and injecting some humour. 'Past Lives' is another hidden gem and more successful than a couple of tracks that made the cut for *Forever Now*. At the time of writing, it's yet to be performed live.

'Play Me' (King/Badarou/P. Gould) 6:04
Originally appearing as an extra track on the 'Forever Now' CD single, this is an intimate funk/pop song kicking off with Mike's very agreeable Wurlitzer electric piano and wah-wah Rhodes. Mark's 'bendy' bass approach is similar to Stanley Clarke's feel on tracks such as 'Journey To Love'. The interesting middle section features Mike overdubbing some rare octave vocals, and he even chimes in with a little spoken French towards the end. 'Play Me' is a minor track, with a verse melody almost identical to 'Forever Now', but it nicely contrasts Mark and Mike's vocal styles. At the time of writing, it has only been performed twice in concert.

'Heart On The Line' (King) 4:50

This track, which appeared as a 'Love In A Peaceful World' B-side and on the 1995 reissue of *Forever Now*, is basically just an infectious, catchy, minimalist groove, but with a pleasingly light touch. Mark's lyric shows sympathy with a young outsider – perhaps drawing on his school experiences – featuring an intriguing reference to 'Brother Al'.

'Time Will Heal' (King/Lindup) 4:07

There's another strong Mike lead vocal on this track which first appeared on the 1995 *Forever Now* re-release. It's a simple song with an attractive melody, catchy string-synth part and nice key-change into the middle section at 2:51. 'Time Will Heal' could almost be an outtake from Mike's *Changes* album and is definitely worth investigating.

'Learn To Say No' (King/Lindup/P. Gould/P. Lorimer) 3:57

This 'All Over You' B-side really is a departure. Featuring elements of house and disco, it wouldn't sound out of place on an M People or Lisa Stansfield album. It foregrounds Bould's excellent conga-playing and showcases another fine Mike lead vocal. Not much is known about one 'P. Lorimer' appearing in the songwriting credits.

'The Bends' (King/Lindup/P Gould) 7:07

A descendant of 'The Sleepwalkers', this is a less-than-essential track that first appeared on the 1995 reissue of *Forever Now*. The intro features lots of drum overdubs from Phil. Mark plays a nice lead guitar line and unleashes some funny falsetto vocals towards the end, but the song lacks a decent melody and meanders along fairly aimlessly. All in all, 'The Bends' definitely screams 'B-side'.

Interlude 1994-2006

The band embarked on a brief UK tour in autumn 1994 to support *Forever Now*. Phil was unwilling to step back into the live arena, so Gavin Harrison was recruited on drums, a highly-respected British session player who had worked with Iggy Pop, Sam Brown, Black, Danny Thompson and many other artists. Jakko returned on guitar, as did the Barnacle/Thirkell horn section (nicknamed The Veterinary Surgeons for the tour!). Very little audio or visual evidence of this period exists except a bootleg recording from Portsmouth Guildhall made on 29 September 1994, available to hear on YouTube. Suddenly BBC Radio 1 were not clamouring for their chance to broadcast a Level gig.

Something had to give. The music industry had completely transformed since their late-1980s heyday, with Britpop now looming large and boybands such as Take That sweeping all before them. The time was right for Level 42 to announce their (temporary) retirement after the last night of the tour at London's Royal Albert Hall on 18 October 1994.

But, as the sporting cliché goes, you're a long time retired. By 1996, Level were almost a distant memory. Guitars were back in vogue big-time, and Britpop bands were referencing acts from the 1960s and 1970s, not the 1980s, which suddenly seemed like the decade that taste forgot. But then, in a curious echo of the original Britfunk movement's 'reaction' to punk, tribute bands began popping up all over England's suburbs and home counties. This rejection of Britpop included tributes to the likes of Madness, Squeeze, The Police, and, of course, Level 42 (this writer played in one such band called Level It Up – read about it in 'True Confessions Of A Tribute Band Drummer' on *movingtheriver.com*). As the 1990s progressed, interest in the band only increased, especially as the chances of a reunion seemed so remote.

Meanwhile, Boon released his debut solo album *Tinman* in 1995. It was a solid selection of mainstream rock songs foregrounding his deep, dark voice and fine guitar playing. It also featured Level tour vocalist Annie McCaig, but failed to find a wide audience.

Mark then issued his second solo album *One Man* on 28 September 1998. It was produced by the little-known Paul Taylor and Boon contributed lyrics for nine out of its ten tracks. Guest musicians included Level regulars Lyndon Connah, Gary Barnacle and Miles Bould, but Mike and Wally were absent. *One Man* focused on Mark's songwriting rather than bass-playing, but was not particularly well-received, failing to chart either in the UK or Europe. Mark then released the *Trash* solo album as a mail-order release in 1999. A cult collection of demos, Level leftovers and experiments, it was sold directly to fans via his website. It was a mixed bag, but featured a couple of minor classics later to become concert regulars: 'Throwing Sevens' and 'Sooner Or Later'.

The mid-to-late 1990s were not kind to Phil. He moved to the middle of Dorset in 1997 to raise his children, but then his marriage ended and his beloved mother Joy passed away late in the decade. It was a difficult period during which music took a back seat.

In 2000, to celebrate the band's 20th anniversary, Polydor issued newly-remastered editions of all Level's studio albums. They appeared in double-CD packs and featured extra tracks and remixes. By 2001, Mark was playing the Royal Albert Hall again as a solo act, with a band that included his younger brother Nathan on guitar and Gary Husband on drums, and his sets were now incorporating an increasing amount of Level material. It seemed the tide was turning again. Mark asked Mike's permission to use the Level 42 name, and Mike generously concurred. The band were back in business. Sean Freeman presently joined on saxophones and Lyndon Connah initially took the keyboard chair.

But the 'reunion' was nearly a very different kettle of fish, as Mark recounted to *Classic Pop* magazine in 2012:

After I acquired the name back in 2002, I tried getting the original line-up back together again to record. I had Phil, Boon, Wally and Mike all sat in my house on the Isle Of Wight, writing some songs. It lasted about four days and then just fell apart. I could see that the old problems and tensions really hadn't gone away. It didn't matter about looking back with rose-tinted spectacles and thinking how wonderful it was. Once you go down a road and you cross some paths, you can't just go back. It's not just a case of rebuilding burned bridges. It's a case of 'that was then and this is now' – things have moved on and changed.

Mike released his second solo album *Conversations With Silence* in November 2003. A collection of instrumental acoustic piano pieces, with the addition of a string quartet, acoustic bass and percussion on a few tracks, it was recorded at his home studio in south-west London. It was a strong release with some excellent playing: 'Brazil 2000' was Mike's most explicitly Latin-influenced track to date. But by the beginning of 2005, Mike had started to miss playing with the band and he came onboard to do the occasional gig, including a reunion of sorts at London's The Forum on 13 February. With Mike's return, it was almost business as usual, and only a matter of time before a new Level 42 album.

Retroglide (2006)

Personnel:
Mark King: Bass Guitar, Percussion, Guitars and Vocals
Mike Lindup: Keyboards and Vocals
Nathan King: Guitars and Vocals
Gary Husband: Drums
Sean Freeman: Saxes
Lyndon Connah: Keyboards
Boon Gould: Guitar
Producer: Mark King
Record Label: W14 Music/Universal
Recorded: The Summerhouse (Isle Of Wight), January-March 2006
Released: 18 September 2006
Running Time: 54:40
Highest Chart Placing: UK: 78, US: –
Current edition: 2013 Level 42 Records

Mike's return to the band in time for *Retroglide* was a huge boon for Mark and long-time Level fans alike. Mark paid tribute to his friend and expanded on their collaboration in an interview with *The Herts Adviser*:

We've spent such a lot of time with each other. Part of the pleasure of working together again is the fact that you really don't have to explain anything. I won't have to say, 'What I'm looking for is this,' because he knows exactly what I'm looking for and vice versa. If he plays something, I can just jump straight in and know exactly what he's thinking and where he's going. You only get that through time, and you don't get a chance to work for 30 years with someone very often. Mike is a far more rounded player than me. He's always working, he's in about fifteen bands, he's just a really strong player and I think that's what he loves to do. And as much as Level 42 is his real baby, it's just one of the bands he plays in.

But though Mike was on great form both vocally and instrumentally, he didn't contribute much keyboard playing to *Retroglide*, and was also entirely absent from the writing credits; Mark composed all the music with Boon emailing lyrics from his Devon home. Wally also didn't contribute to the album, busy with his soundtrack work and solo career.

The result was a fairly introspective, relatively downbeat album, with lots of tracks in a similar 'rock ballad' style. Sadly, the songs generally lacked character or a dramatic conceit that might provide a little relief or even novelty factor, in the way that 'The Sun Goes Down' and 'The Chinese Way' somehow tapped into the zeitgeist. But, on the plus side, Mark was making great strides as a singer and was much more experimental and ambitious with his vocals this time around.

One digital single was released from the album, and a four-track preview CD was sent out to radio stations and print publications. *Retroglide*'s impressive cover was designed by Alan Brooks, who had worked on the sleeves for 'The Chinese Way' and 'Out of Sight, Out of Mind'. The band toured extensively to promote the album, with Mike once again announced as a permanent member in May 2006, replacing Lyndon Connah.

'Dive Into The Sun' (King/R. Gould) 4:03

Kicking off with Mark's favourite Mahavishnu-style arpeggios – reminiscent of the tracks 'The Dance Of Maya' and 'Vision Is An Emerald Beyond' – 'Dive Into The Sun' develops into a superior slice of funk/rock with wicked Mike Rhodes-comping and excellent Chick Corea-style runs at 1:26 and 2:47. There's also a brief but expressive sax solo from Freeman. The song showcases an incredibly tight band sound, but the mix is airless and claustrophobic, with Gary's drums in particular lacking character. But, in general, aided by Boon's powerful lyric, 'Dive Into The Sun' is a welcome return for the band, and was included as part of a four-track *Retroglide* preview CD.

'Rooted' (King/R. Gould) 5:35

Kicking off with Nathan's guitar harmonics, 'Rooted' develops into a classic Level half-time groove, with a fine synth bassline and treated Husband drums. The verse melody is attractive, underpinned by a beguiling mixture of major and minor chords, but the chorus is fairly unmemorable. Mike inserts some potent synths and plays an excellent solo, while Mark comes up with some great vocal improvisations including some of his highest notes on record. Boon supplies an impressive lyric with no wasted phrases, perhaps a rumination on his Isle Of Wight childhood.

'The Way Back Home' (King/R. Gould) 6:55

'The Way Back Home' was the sole (digital-only) single released from *Retroglide*, also included on the four-track preview CD. Mark embellishes the very simple verse G/D/C chord sequence with some tasty harmonics, but his melody lacks variety. There's a nice modulation and surprising change into a major key, and Mike adds some novel, Scritti Politti-style rhythm synths. Boon's lyric seems to be a plea for anonymity. 'The Way Back Home' is fairly catchy, but the track's chugging mid-tempo rock isn't really anyone's idea of an essential Level 42 groove.

'Just For You' (King/R. Gould) 4:54

Mark dips into the Todd Rundgren songbook again for this downbeat, rather repetitive ballad. Gary plays an interesting half-time groove, but the song is mainly centred around Mike's keyboard embellishments on piano and synth. The chorus flits between minor/major chords in the manner of 'Take A Look', while Mike delivers some striking falsetto harmonies towards the end. But in the final analysis, a good band performance and strong vocal can't save this one. 'Just For You' was one of the tracks on the four-song CD sent out to preview the album.

'Sleep Talking' (King/R. Gould) 5:02

This is classic late-period Level, a mash-up of 'Fashion Fever' and 'The Sunbed Song'. A complex arrangement gives lots of room for Gary to express himself on the drums. Mark double-tracks his bass during the intro, concluding with an extravagant flamenco-style flourish, and later unleashes some classic Jaco-style sixteenth notes. Mike adds lovely Rhodes comping throughout, and Freeman also gets some rare solo space. Intense and turbo-charged, 'Sleep Talking' is one of the more successful tracks on *Retroglide*.

'Retroglide' (King/R. Gould) 4:51

The album's title track is a rather underwhelming 'rock' ballad, closer to Elbow than Earth, Wind & Fire, and mainly a vehicle for Nathan's guitar: he adds an excellent solo and also supplies neat pedal-steel effects throughout. Mark delivers a fine vocal and decent chorus, but, uncharacteristically, Gary overplays a little. In general, the song has an unfinished quality and could possibly have been improved by a subtler treatment.

'All Around' (King/R. Gould) 5:02

Mark's opening bass runs sound uncannily like Stanley Clarke (the rest of the track features two basslines, one on the five-string and the other on the four) and then we hear the album's now-overly-familiar half-time groove. The verse features a modal melody over some pretty static chords: always a tricky thing to pull off, but it just about holds the attention. Freeman then solos strongly but the track ends pretty abruptly. 'All Around' is certainly one of the least memorable songs in the Level catalogue. Lyrically, it seems to be another of Boon's pops at the 'celeb' lifestyle ('Don't like your TV-ocracy/Your karaoke-osophy').

'Clouds' (King/R. Gould) 4:33

It's ballad time again, this time in a rare 6/8 time signature. The verse features some pretty chords and subtle Rhodes-playing from Mike. Nathan delivers an excellent guitar solo in the American 'session' style, a la Toto's Steve Lukather. Mike's harmony vocals during the refrain are very welcome, making one wish he had featured a little more on the album. 'Clouds' was featured on the four-track album preview sent out in advance of *Retroglide*.

'Hell Town Story' (King/R. Gould) 4:58

'Hell Town Story' is another fairly standard Level groove, but a highlight of *Retroglide* in terms of everything hanging together well and its refreshingly 'bluesy' feel. Mark doubles his bass again and kicks in with a great vamp after the second chorus. The lyric seems to be a gently satirical poke at the mega-rich, with a subtly ominous pay-off line: 'It's gonna end all by itself'.

'Ship' (King/R. Gould) 5:14

This was the last Level 42 track to feature input from all four founder members. It's yet another ballad, but an ambitious song featuring the intelligent, unmistakable arrangement ideas of an uncredited Phil. Boon contributes lyrics and plays an excellent, cascading guitar solo, only making one wonder what might have been if he'd been persuaded to play on the album a little more. Lyrically, 'Ship' is a clever extension of a simple metaphor, exploring the consequences of the aphorism 'Be careful what you wish for':

> When your ship comes in
> Will you step onboard with a smile
> Or will they have to press-gang you?

Affecting and subtle, 'Ship' is a real *Retroglide* standout, benefitting hugely from Phil's contribution.

'All I Need' (King/R Gould) 5:26

There are more Mahavishnu-style games from Mark on this 6/8 album-closer, loosely based on the 'Meeting Of The Spirits' riff. His vocal range is impressive and he plays what sounds like a brief piccolo bass solo at 2:46. The last-minute of the track features some uncharacteristically fast keyboard licks from Mike, on acoustic piano and Rhodes. 'All I Need' is not a brilliant song by any means, but Level are the only band who could have come up with it.

Interlude (2007-2012)

Level toured extensively to support *Retroglide*, with British and European gigs during late 2006. But the following year was a quiet one for the band, with just a handful of concerts. Gary was then unable to make a few performances during 2008, having already committed to working with John McLaughlin, so he suggested a pretty formidable 'dep': the one and only Billy Cobham. Cobham accepted an invitation to join Level 42 at the North Sea Jazz Festival in The Hague, Netherlands, on 24 May 2008. It was a huge honour for Mark and Mike, Mark later telling *Jazzwise* magazine:

> Gary suggested I give Bill a call, and what do you know, he said yes! It was quite something standing in rehearsals looking at your hero sitting behind the drums and playing your songs. Surreal doesn't come close.

Kicking off with 'Foundation & Empire', it was a memorable set of music for band and fans alike. (Mark, Mike, Nathan and Sean Freeman later returned the favour and joined Cobham during his Ronnie Scott's residency in February 2015.)

Meanwhile, Phil had been steadily returning to drumming throughout the 2000s, after moving back to London and playing some well-received club gigs (this writer recalls seeing him with Gary Barnacle at The Sugar Hut in Fulham circa 2006). He was also composing a lot of music and finally released his debut solo album *Watertight* in 2009. Wally was Phil's chief collaborator, mostly exchanging audio files by email, later telling *Classic Pop* magazine:

> Phil and I remained close throughout the years, enough to trust each other when working from a distance. I was happy to help him deliver his first solo effort. We didn't worry whether it was going to be too Level 42-ish, we just performed it as we felt. It's an album I'm really proud of.

Mike was ever-present on vocals and keyboards, delivering great performances on the standouts 'Cool Man Yeah' and 'Colour Of My Pain'. *Watertight* also featured vocalist Berenice Scott, daughter of Robin. In October 2020, Phil announced that he would soon be releasing his second solo album.

The Level 42 back catalogue was given a boost in July 2010 when Universal Music released the *Living It Up* box set, comprising all of the band's singles, some rarities, live tracks and a whole disc of acoustic reversions. Mark told *The Herts Adviser* more about how the acoustic tracks came about:

> The acoustic album came about as a case of 'needs-must', because when we were out doing the *Retroglide* tour in 2006, we were doing a lot of radio. They were always saying, 'Bring a couple of guitars and play some songs for us'. I explained that there's no slap bass involved in acoustic music and this was something completely alien to us, so we lost the promotion. So the third time I brought a guitar along, Mike brought his electric piano and off we went.

There just happened to be one thing called 'All I Need', off *Retroglide*, which really did lend itself to an acoustic version, so that made sense, but while we were there they said 'Play 'Lessons In Love', and you think 'Oh, bloody hell'! So we just bluffed our way through a couple of radio sessions. Then, because it was on the website, people starting saying 'It sounds really good, do you have any plans to release it?', and we said, 'Oh yes, we intend to make a whole acoustic album, any minute now'! Four years later, I'm talking to Universal and they're looking for stuff for this box set, so I said 'What about this mythical acoustic album?', and they said 'OK'. When you deconstruct these songs and put them back together, you can sort of mess about with the melodies, find some really dark corners and turn them on their heads. I also think they were good songs to begin with, and it's very hard to muck them up!

Gary officially left Level 42 for the second and last time in 2010, joining his Mahavishnu hero John McLaughlin's 4th Dimension band. He recorded and toured extensively with the guitar master, playing both keyboards and drums on the albums *To The One*, *Now Here This*, *Black Light*, *Live At Ronnie Scott's* and *Live In San Francisco*. At the time of writing, Gary has also recorded six solo collections, including the critically-acclaimed *The Things I See* and *A Meeting Of Spirits*, inspired by the music of Allan Holdsworth and McLaughlin respectively.

But then the question arose as to who would take Gary's place in Level 42. It was definitely one of the most desirable drumming gigs in British music. Mark and Mike could probably have had their pick of any player. Eventually the spotlight fell on precociously-talented, Sheffield-born Pete Ray Biggin, who had first played with Level at the age of just eleven. Mark told *The Herts Adviser* more about Biggin's recruitment:

The drumming agency told me to have a look at this clip of this guy Pete on YouTube, so I gave him a call and he said he was a big fan of the band. So I said that's very nice of you to say that, mate - do you fancy coming along and having a crack, because we've got a load of shows coming up, and he said he'd love to. So we got together in London and ran through some stuff, and he really does know it inside and out, the guy fits in a treat. Afterwards, he said to me, 'I don't know if you remember, but in 1990 when you did the *Guaranteed* tour, you came to Leeds University and my parents brought me along to the soundcheck – I was eleven years old and you let me get up and I jammed three songs with you'. He sent me all these photographs of him on Gary's drums, and it was amazing because he was like this young prodigy, and he'd obviously been a fan of the band and aspired to be a good musician and here he is today – he's part of Mark Ronson's thing, he works with Amy Winehouse, and he's with Incognito. The guy's never stopped working.

Meanwhile, Mike issued his third solo album *On The One* on 17 March 2011, a self-released collection of vocal tracks with guest players including Dominic

Miller, Miles Bould, bassist Yolanda Charles and vocalist Sumudu. During the 2010s, Mike also toured and recorded extensively as part of Miller's band.

In February 2012, Mark gathered Mike, Gary, Pete, Nathan, Sean Freeman and various other renowned British session players at Ronnie Scott's to play his *Influences* album in its entirety. It was a spellbinding evening of music and a timely reminder of Mark's jazz/rock roots.

Level then toured extensively to support the 25th anniversary of *Running In The Family*, easily their biggest-selling album. A new Super Deluxe Edition featured a whole disc of acoustic reversions. In October 2012, Boon was a special guest during Mark's birthday gig in Reading, England, playing a typically impressive solo during 'Heathrow'. It would be his last ever live appearance with the band. The European tour also included Level's first gig at Amsterdam's Paradiso for 31 years, an emotional moment for both Mike and Mark, as the Netherlands had always been their biggest market outside the UK. Mike reviewed the concert for *Classic Pop* magazine: 'We eschewed the usual handshakes for proper man-hugs: it had been one of those special moments which will forever be saved in the memory banks...'.

So even though Level 42 were still a potent live act in 2012, one could be forgiven for thinking they were a spent force in terms of recording. But then ...

Sirens EP (2013)

Personnel:
Mark King: Bass and Lead Vocals
Mike Lindup: Keyboards and Vocals
Pete Ray Biggin: Drums and Percussion
Nathan King: Guitar
Sean Freeman: Saxophone
Producer: John Morales
Engineer: John Morales
Record Label: Level 42 Records
Recorded: The Summerhouse (Isle Of Wight), 2013
Released: 2013
Running Time: 38:88
Highest Chart Placing: UK: -, US: -
Current edition: 2016 Level 42 Records

By the early 2010s, Mark was listening to more contemporary music than he had since the 1980s. He was a fan of artists such as Elbow, Everything Everything, CeeLo Green and Aloe Blacc, and found himself sufficiently inspired to write a new collection of songs. The resulting EP *Sirens* was to some extent a return to the band's roots – an era when 'dance music' equalled grooves that had swing and space – and also featured influences from funk, jazz, soul and Latin. Mark wasn't interested in competing with his illustrious back catalogue though – it was just an excuse to have some fun and create some new material to play live.

The result was six lengthy tracks with long, slowly-building introductions, seductive grooves and no rush to get to the pop hooks. The aim for *Sirens* may have been modest, but it ended up being a huge improvement on *Retroglide*, not least because the mix is spacious and the music possesses an easy swagger. Mike was in his element too with the EP's emphasis on old-school synths and dawn-of-the-'80s grooves. Biggin made a fine recording debut with the band, totally at home and getting plenty of space to show off his quite considerable chops. Wally, though, was sadly once again absent.

A recommendation from Universal Music led Mark to Bronx-born DJ and mixer John Morales, who was sent the audio stems for the tracks and then 'remixed' them as if they were twelve-inch singles. Mark liked the mixes so much that he decided to release them exactly as they were.

Sirens was released on the newly-established Level 42 Records. Mark had suddenly found himself both band manager and label boss, telling *Classic Pop* magazine:

I went and had a chat with the major labels, but I felt they weren't going to do anything I couldn't do myself. They just want access to your database and Facebook (friends). So I've become my own little fat label producer! I wish I'd done it sooner. EPs are the way to go.

It seemed to work: the *Sirens* EP was widely reported as a return to form and even received a five-star review in *Blues & Soul* magazine.

The band toured extensively to support the release, spending autumn and winter 2013 on the road in the UK and Europe, the horn section bolstered by two new players: trombonist Nicholl Thompson and trumpeter Dan Carpenter. An impressive double-CD and DVD was also released to commemorate the *Sirens* tour, released in 2015.

'Sirens' (King) 6:33

The EP's title track is a big burst of summery, retro fun, featuring a four-on-the-floor kick drum, satisfying chord sequence and typical Mark slap-and-tickle bassline. He even attempts a bit of a rap, followed by an expansive solo section with lots of cool jazz chord changes and a strong tenor feature from Sean Freeman, very much under the influence of Michael Brecker. In 2013, a new Level EP wasn't going to change the music world, but it was a very pleasant surprise to hear such a classy, committed performance as this.

'Too Much Time' (King) 6:17

This was a return to the kind of half-time shuffle last heard on 'One In A Million', and it's a definite *Sirens* standout. Mark plays two basslines with a fatter tone than usual. Biggin impresses with slick hi-hat work in the right channel and introduces some enjoyably crazy fills, increasing in intensity as the piece develops. The refrain is very much influenced by Sly & The Family Stone, maybe inspired by Mark's guest spot with that band's legendary bassist Larry Graham at London's Jazz Café on 3 March 2013. Lyrically, it's quite refreshing to hear Mark letting off some steam about his creative and personal *ennui* on this song, and it certainly sounds like he means it. He performed 'Too Much Time' for one of his regular Covid-19 'lockdown' live tracks posted on YouTube during May 2020.

'Mind On You' (King) 8:38

'Mind On You' kicks off with a killer Latin/funk groove, a sprightly Mark finger-style bassline and modal strings very influenced by the Marvin Gaye/Donny Hathaway school, with shades of 'Romance' from *Forever Now*. Mike chimes in with some funky Fender Rhodes and even an old-school Vocoder. Biggin gets some space to let his hair down at around the six-minute mark, delivering a great drum feature alongside Nathan's choppy rhythm guitar. 'Mind On You' is another infectious track, and has become somewhat of a live favourite.

'My Independence Day' (King) 6:11

This is Mark's homage to the Jon Anderson and Vangelis composition 'State Of Independence', taken into the UK singles chart by Donna Summer in 1982. He lays down his version of the famous rolling bass riff (in G, whereas Summer's version is in B) over a fat drum-machine beat. Mike delivers his first lead vocal of the album – his slow-moving, modal top-line wouldn't sound out of place on a Santana or Leon Thomas album, especially given its lyrical theme of 'The Love Divine'; you can almost imagine the excellent 'My Independence Day' rebooted as a spiritual jazz tune.

'Build Myself A Rocket' (King) 6:38

'Build Myself A Rocket' features an interesting lopsided groove with a great bassline and old-school synth sound. Mark double-tracks his vocals in the first verse, and then he's joined by daughter Marlee in the second. The lyrics are amusingly anodyne, but everyone sounds like they're having a great time. The weakest track on *Sirens*, 'Build Myself A Rocket' has nevertheless become a live favourite for the band.

'Where's Yo' Head At?' (King) 5:51

It's interesting that the title references a Basement Jaxx tune – maybe it's a backhanded compliment to the British dance act for the distinctly Mark-like slap-bass sample (actually a sample of 'Far Beyond' by Locksmith) that featured on their 1999 hit 'Red Alert'. Biggin kicks off with a great timbale solo, and Mike's synth refrain references the outro of 'Starchild'. The song's chord sequence owes a lot to Ronnie Laws' 1975 jazz/funk classic 'Always There'. With its excellent horn arrangements and manic energy, 'Where's Yo' Head At?' is a decent closer for the EP, and typical of the band's funk/rock sound throughout the 2010s.

Postscript

In the years following the release of *Sirens*, the band's live schedule showed no signs of letting up. They were still selling out concert halls all over Europe and also challenging themselves by playing festival gigs to audiences who didn't necessarily know their material.

Meanwhile, Phil continued his return to live performance during the 2010s, playing several London gigs and appearing with Mike and Wally at the 606 Club on 11 January 2016. Mike maintained his collaboration with Dominic Miller and also performed occasionally as a solo headliner, sometimes with Phil on drums and Wally on keyboards too. When not on tour with Level, Pete Ray Biggin developed his solo project The PB Underground, a collective of London musicians and vocalists fusing funk, soul, jazz and R&B. Meanwhile, Nathan King joined neo-prog bands It Bites and Frost*.

Mark kept himself busy too, working with the Nordoff Robbins charity and becoming a regular face at the London Bass Guitar Shows at the Olympia Centre, including a memorable event in March 2015 when he signed autographs and swapped stories with fans for hours, holding court in his inimitable way. In March 2016, he received a text from ex-Police drummer Stewart Copeland: 'Hey Mark, wanna come and record an album in Florence?'. It was an offer he couldn't refuse, and he joined Copeland, ex-King Crimson guitarist/vocalist Adrian Belew and keyboardist/songwriter Vittorio Cosma to record the album *Gizmodrome*. Released on 15 September 2017, it was a quirky set of avant-rock songs which saw Mark contributing some vocals and experimenting with bass tones and techniques.

Level 42 then gathered again to embark on *The Eternity Tour* during autumn 2018. An excellent Brighton Dome gig on 24 October was captured and released on DVD, including a superb revamped version of 'The Machine Stops'.

As 2020 dawned, Mark entered a new decade very happy with his place in the musical lexicon, and also happy to be chiefly known for his 1980s work: 'It would be odd if Connan Mockasin or Christine And The Queens were to get on the phone and say, "Mark, can you come and ruin my record for me by slapping all over it for no reason?"', he told the *WORD* podcast with typical self-effacement in 2018. 'I'm of my time, but we wrote some great songs too.' And, helped by the streaming revolution at the time of writing, it seems as if the Level 42 catalogue is attracting a whole new generation of fans (including this writer's teenage niece).

The band's 40th anniversary *From Eternity To Here* tour was originally set for summer 2020, but the Covid-19 crisis put paid to that. At the time of writing, all live dates have been rescheduled for autumn 2021, and the fun looks set to continue. Mark is now the gatekeeper of the Level 42 brand – label manager and tour manager – but remains disarmingly modest about his career and the band's progress since 1980: 'When I look back now at photographs from that period of time, I still see the kid in me who was just winging it', he told *The Greatest Music Of All Time* YouTube channel in 2020. Phil also summed it all up very well onstage at the 606 Club on 12 October 2017: 'Even though things ended in a way we'd rather they didn't, we're still brothers in arms, and we'll always be that to our dying day'.

Selected Official Compilations/Box Sets

Level Best (1989)
The Remixes (1992)
The Very Best Of Level 42 (1998)
The Definitive Collection (2006)
Weave Your Spell: The Collection (2007)
Past Lives: The Best Of The RCA Years (2007)
Living It Up (2010)
The Ultimate Collection (2017)

Selected Official DVDs/Videos

Live At Wembley (1987)

Level's first officially released video, this was a crucial artefact of the band's commercial peak, filmed at London's Wembley Arena on 1 December 1986. It's an irresistible juggernaut of pop/funk hooks and great tunes. It's also a real treat to see Phil firing on all cylinders, perched behind his famous yellow Tama kit in Hawaiian shirt and shades. The tracks that hit the cutting-room floor (but available to hear on YouTube) are 'The Chant Has Begun', 'I Want Eyes', 'Micro Kid', 'Running In The Family' (with Phil's original lyrics) and 'Are You Hearing (What I Hear)?'.

Level Best (1989)

Level's first video collection brought together most of the promos from their first decade, plus a performance of 'Love Games' from *Top Of The Pops* in April 1981. It's an uneven selection, from the excellent ('Something About You', 'Take Care Of Yourself') to the risible ('The Chant Has Begun'), and probably now only of interest to completists.

Fait Accompli (1989)

This documentary, following the band through the four-month *Staring At The Sun* world tour, is a superb look at the state of the global pop industry at the end of the 1980s and an absolute must for any Level fan (this writer rushed out to buy it on the day of release). It shows the band sound-checking, travelling between hotels, hanging out on video/photo shoots and killing time in dressing rooms. And of course, there's a lot of excellent live footage from the European tour. Mark is an oasis of calm in the middle of all this craziness: sober, jovial, quoting from *This Is Spinal Tap*, telling his famous 'bass solo' joke and revelling in the band's peak popularity. *Q Magazine* co-founder/*Whistle Test* presenter David Hepworth is our tour guide and 'Englishman abroad', grabbing interviews with Mark, Mike, Alan Murphy, Gary and Paul Crockford (who becomes a bit of a star of the doc with his constant wisecracks, odd asides and deafening suits) along the way.

Fait Accompli also mercilessly puts the corporate wonks under the spotlight: it's squeaky-bum time for Head of Polydor UK David Munns, Senior Marketing Manager Mark Foster and Video Manager Chris Johnson, with the label demanding Stateside hits. We see the making of the 'Heaven In My Hands' and 'Take A Look' videos, and there's a horrible irony when Johnson explains his concept of giving the Americans 'something they can't refuse', given the subsequent total failure of both singles in the USA. But such was the precarious nature of the music business in the late 1980s. The essential *Fait Accompli* DVD is currently available as part of the *Running In The Family Super Deluxe Edition* box set.

Guaranteed Live (1992)

Recorded at London's Town & Country Club on 20 March 1992, this is a well-shot document of a relatively intimate gig featuring Jakko on guitar, Gary on drums, Annie McCaig on vocals and the Barnacle/Thirkell horn section. It's a nicely-paced set with lots of tracks from *Guaranteed*, plus Mike's 'The Spirit Is Free' and spectacular versions of 'Mr Pink' and 'The Chinese Way'. It also features arguably the best-ever vocals on a Level 42 tour, with Jakko's voice working superbly with Mike, Mark and McCaig. It's only slightly marred by a muddy drum sound, too many Jakko solos and Gary's dodgy vest and headband, but *Guaranteed Live* is still pretty essential viewing.

At Rockpalast (2005)

This is an excellent double-disc set comprising two complete German *Rockpalast* concerts from 1983 and 1984. The former features epic versions of 'Sandstorm', 'Are You Hearing (What I Hear)?' and 'Starchild' (with Mark indulging in some amusing Max Wall-style dancing), while the latter showcases a key date from the *True Colours* tour. DVD extras include a funny band interview and an impromptu *a cappella* vocal. Essential stuff.

Live From Metropolis Studios DVD (2012)

This is a fine document of a fan-club-only gig from the recording studio/ rehearsal space in Chiswick, West London, taped on 10 December 2011. It's all good fun and a great chance to see the band in an intimate setting, with Mark in fine form and a solid performance of all the hits, including a drastically reworked 'Hot Water' featuring some quotes from 'Return Of The Handsome Rugged Man'. The DVD also showcases some interesting, rarely-played album tracks such as 'Romance', 'Lying Still' and 'True Believers'.

Selected Online/TV/Radio References:

level42.com
mikelindup.com
philgouldmusic.com
garyhusband.com
peteraybiggin.com
seanfreemanmusic.com
wallybadarou.com

BBC Sight And Sound In Concert (1983)
Recorded at The Regal, Hitchin, UK, on 16 February 1983

Live In Montreux (1983)
Recorded at the *Montreux Jazz Festival* on 13 July 1983

BBC In Concert: Live At The Brixton Ace (1983)
Recorded at the London venue (currently named The Brixton Academy) on 25 November 1983

Play At Home BBC documentary (1984)
https://www.youtube.com/watch?v=FXV99VhXlVs
A great documentary shot in autumn 1983 and broadcast on Channel 4 during summer 1984, including footage of the band's October 1983 gig at the Hammersmith Odeon in London. The film focuses on music education and Level's Isle Of Wight background, and includes amusing live versions of the *Hawaii Five-O* theme song and 'Tie A Yellow Ribbon Round The Ole Oak Tree'. Other episodes of *Play At Home*, also shown throughout summer 1984, featured XTC, New Order, Echo & The Bunnymen and Siouxsie and The Banshees.

Mark King: *My Top Ten* BBC Radio 1 interview (14 July 1984)
Mark King: *The Stereo Sequence* BBC Radio 1 interview (March 1987)
Mark King: *The Way It Is* Capital Radio interview (1991)
Level 42 *Music Box* interview (1991): https://www.youtube.com/watch?v=D7s1JKO9D1g
Mark King *King Of The Isle* interview (1996): https://www.youtube.com/watch?v=bb3KND8W-Wg
Level 42 *MCM* interview (1992): https://www.youtube.com/watch?v=IjA4vhXzBFc
Superstar DJs: The Funk Mafia documentary (2000): https://www.youtube.com/watch?v=zkQT8JVEPH0
Phil Gould *Inside MusiCast* interview (2013): https://www.insidemusicast.com/musicasts/2013/5/13/phil-gould.html

Phil Gould *speedgig.com* interview (2014): https://www.youtube.com/ watch?v=7P_6blWUiXI

WORD podcast featuring Mark King in conversation with Mark Ellen and David Hepworth (September 2018): http://wordpodcast.co.uk/2018/09/20/word-podcast-290-mark-king-on-forty-years-of-funk/

Gary Husband *Inside MusiCast* interview (2019): https://www.insidemusicast. com/musicasts/2019/18/10-gary-husband

Mark King: *Tracks Of My Years* BBC Radio 2 (February 2020): https://www. youtube.com/watch?v=Tk9W1t0t8N4
Mark's choices:
The Hollies: 'He Ain't Heavy, He's My Brother'
Scritti Politti: 'The Word Girl'
Roxy Music: 'Avalon'
The Police: 'Spirits In The Material World'
Patsy Cline: 'Sweet Dreams'
Sly & The Family Stone: 'Thank You (Falettinme Be Mice Elf Agin)'
Queen/David Bowie: 'Under Pressure'
Amy Winehouse: 'Love Is A Losing Game'
XTC: 'Making Plans For Nigel'
Golden Earring: 'Radar Love'

Mark King *The Greatest Music Of All Time* interview (April 2020):
https://www.youtube.com/watch?v=F0RuwjofCk4

Gary Husband *DrumTalkTV* interview (May 2020):
https://www.youtube.com/watch?v=nXtRiwWzpkU

Mark King *Suzi Perry Breakfast Club* interview (May 2020):
https://www.youtube.com/watch?v=KGk_wRdo5QQ

Mike Lindup *Professor Of Rock* interview (July 2020):
https://www.youtube.com/watch?v=vqk2RJjGA38

This page: Mark, Mike, Phil and Boon featured in the (almost) black and while sequences in the 'Something About You' video.

Right: Mike and Boon on *Top Of The Pops* in January 1983.

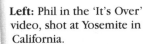

Left: Phil in the 'It's Over' video, shot at Yosemite in California.

Right: Mark at Wembley Arena in 1989.

This page: Three Level 42 twelve-inch singles: 'The Sun Goes Down (Livin' It Up)' from 1983, 'Hot Water' from 1984 and 'Tracie' from 1989.

Bibliography

Reynolds, S., *Rip It Up And Start Again Postpunk 1978-1984* (Faber & Faber, 2006)

Reynolds, S., *Totally Wired: Post-Punk Interviews And Overviews* (Faber & Faber, 2009)

Cowton, M., *Level 42* (Sidgwick & Jackson, 1989)

Garfield, S., *Expensive Habits: The Dark Side Of The Music Industry* (Faber & Faber, 1986)

Dolby, T., *The Speed Of Sound: Breaking The Barriers Between Music And Technology* (Flatiron Books, 2016)

Cunningham, M., *Good Vibrations: A History Of Record Production* (Sanctuary Publishing, 1999)

Lawrence, T., *Life And Death On The NYC Dancefloor 1980-1983* (Duke University Press, 2016)

Patterson, S., *I'm Not With The Band* (Sphere, 2016)

Zollo, P., *More Songwriters On Songwriting* (Da Capo Press, 2016)

Doyle, T., *The Glamour Chase: The Maverick Life Of Billy Mackenzie* (Bloomsbury, 1998)

Scott, K., *Abbey Road To Ziggy Stardust: My Autobiography* (Alfred Publishing, 2012)

Koestler, A., *The Invisible Writing* (Vintage Classics, 2005)

Forster, E.M., *The Machine Stops* (Penguin Modern Classics, 2011)

Packard, R., *The Kansas City Milkman* (Dutton, 1950)

Asimov, I., *Foundation And Empire* (Harper Voyager, 2016)

Adams, D., *The Hitchhiker's Guide To The Galaxy* (Pan, 2020)

Jung, C.G., *Memories, Dreams, Reflections* (Flamingo, 1995)

Hesse, H., *The Prodigy* (Peter Owen Publishers, 2011)

Brown, P., *Are We Still Rolling?* (Tape Op, 2010)

Waller, P., *Level 42: The Worldwide Visual Discography* (Paul Waller/Level 42 Records, 2017)

Ondaatje, M., *Running In The Family* (Bloomsbury, 2009)

Barnes, J., *Staring At The Sun* (Vintage, 2009)

Herbert, F., *Dune* (Hodder, 2015)

Matheson, R., *I Am Legend* (Macmillan, 2007)

On Track series

Barclay James Harvest – Keith and Monica Domone 978-1-78952-

The Beatles – Andrew Wild 978-1-78952-009-5

The Beatles Solo 1969-1980 – Andrew Wild 978-1-78952-030-9

Blue Oyster Cult – Jacob Holm-Lupo 978-1-78952-007-1

Kate Bush – Bill Thomas 978-1-78952-097-2

The Clash – Nick Assirati 978-1-78952-077-4

Crosby, Stills and Nash – Andrew Wild 978-1-78952-039-2

Deep Purple and Rainbow 1968-79 – Steve Pilkington 978-1-78952-002-6

Dire Straits – Andrew Wild 978-1-78952-044-6

Dream Theater – Jordan Blum 978-1-78952-050-7

Emerson Lake and Palmer – Mike Goode 978-1-78952-000-2

Fairport Convention – Kevan Furbank 978-1-78952-051-4

Genesis – Stuart MacFarlane 978-1-78952-005-7

Gentle Giant – Gary Steel 978-1-78952-058-3

Hawkwind – Duncan Harris 978-1-78952-052-1

Iron Maiden – Steve Pilkington 978-1-78952-061-3

Jethro Tull – Jordan Blum 978-1-78952-016-3

Elton John in the 1970s – Peter Kearns 978-1-78952-034-7

Gong – Kevan Furbank 978-1-78952-082-8

Iron Maiden – Steve Pilkington 978-1-78952-061-3

Judas Priest – John Tucker 978-1-78952-018-7

Kansas – Kevin Cummings 978-1-78952-057-6

Aimee Mann – Jez Rowden 978-1-78952-036-1

Joni Mitchell – Peter Kearns 978-1-78952-081-1

The Moody Blues – Geoffrey Feakes 978-1-78952-042-2

Mike Oldfield – Ryan Yard 978-1-78952-060-6

Queen – Andrew Wild 978-1-78952-003-3

Renaissance – David Detmer 978-1-78952-062-0

The Rolling Stones 1963-80 – Steve Pilkington 978-1-78952-017-0

Steely Dan – Jez Rowden 978-1-78952-043-9

Thin Lizzy – Graeme Stroud 978-1-78952-064-4

Toto – Jacob Holm-Lupo 978-1-78952-019-4

U2 – Eoghan Lyng 978-1-78952-078-1

UFO – Richard James 978-1-78952-073-6

The Who – Geoffrey Feakes 978-1-78952-076-7

Roy Wood and the Move – James R Turner 978-1-78952-008-8

Van Der Graaf Generator – Dan Coffey 978-1-78952-031-6

Yes – Stephen Lambe 978-1-78952-001-9

Frank Zappa 1966 to 1979 – Eric Benac 978-1-78952-033-0

10CC – Peter Kearns 978-1-78952-054-5

Decades Series
Pink Floyd In The 1970s – Georg Purvis 978-1-78952-072-9
Marillion in the 1980s – Nathaniel Webb 978-1-78952-065-1

On Screen series
Carry On... – Stephen Lambe 978-1-78952-004-0
David Cronenberg – Patrick Chapman 978-1-78952-071-2
Doctor Who: The David Tennant Years – Jamie Hailstone 978-1-78952-066-8
Monty Python – Steve Pilkington 978-1-78952-047-7
Seinfeld Seasons 1 to 5 – Stephen Lambe 978-1-78952-012-5

Other Books
Derek Taylor: For Your Radioactive Children – Andrew Darlington
978-1-78952-
Jon Anderson and the Warriors - the road to Yes – David Watkinson
978-1-78952-059-0
Tommy Bolin: In and Out of Deep Purple – Laura Shenton
978-1-78952-070-5
Maximum Darkness – Deke Leonard 978-1-78952-048-4
Maybe I Should've Stayed In Bed – Deke Leonard 978-1-78952-053-8
The Twang Dynasty – Deke Leonard 978-1-78952-049-1

and many more to come!

Would you like to write for Sonicbond Publishing?

We are mainly a music publisher, but we also occasionally publish in other genres including film and television. At Sonicbond Publishing we are always on the look-out for authors, particularly for our two main series, On Track and Decades.

Mixing fact with in depth analysis, the On Track series examines the entire recorded work of a particular musical artist or group. All genres are considered from easy listening and jazz to 60s soul to 90s pop, via rock and metal.

The Decades series singles out a particular decade in an artist or group's history and focuses on that decade in more detail than may be allowed in the On Track series.

While professional writing experience would, of course, be an advantage, the most important qualification is to have real enthusiasm and knowledge of your subject. First-time authors are welcomed, but the ability to write well in English is essential.

Sonicbond Publishing has distribution throughout Europe and North America, and all our books are also published in E-book form. Authors will be paid a royalty based on sales of their book. Further details about our books are available from www.sonicbondpublishing.com. To contact us, complete the contact form there or email info@sonicbondpublishing.co.uk